CRANBORNE CHASE

A SECRET LANDSCAPE

ROGER LANE

Photography by Roger Lane & Roger Holman

AMBERLEY

Dedicated to Rosemary (Ro) Holman

(1937–2014)

First published 2015

Amberley Publishing
The Hill, Stroud, Gloucestershire, GL5 4EP
www.amberley-books.com

Copyright © Roger Lane and Roger Holman, 2015

The right of Roger Lane and Roger Holman to be identified as the Author of this work has been asserted in accordance with the Copyrights, Designs and Patents Act 1988.

ISBN 978 1 4456 4984 9 (print)
ISBN 978 1 4456 4985 6 (ebook)

British Library Cataloguing in Publication Data.
A catalogue record for this book is available from the British Library.

Typesetting by Amberley Publishing.
Printed in the UK.

CONTENTS

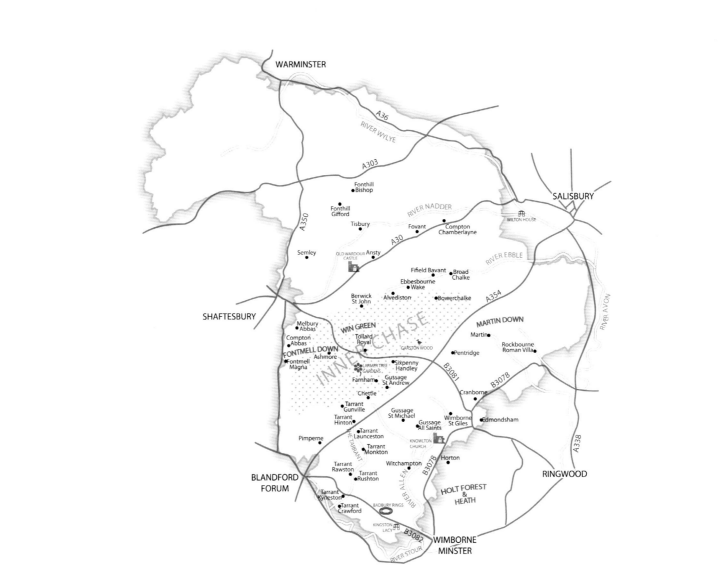

WARMINSTER

A36

RIVER WYLYE

A303

Fonthill
Bishop

RIVER NADDER

SALISBURY

Fonthill
Gifford

Tisbury

Fovant

Compton
Chamberlayne

WILTON HOUSE

A350

A30

RIVER EBBLE

Semley

OLD WARDOUR
CASTLE

Ansty

Fifield Bavant

Broad
Chalke

Ebbesbourne
Wake

SHAFTESBURY

Berwick
St John

Alvediston

Bowerchalke

A354

RIVER AVON

Melbury
Abbas

WIN GREEN

MARTIN DOWN

Compton
Abbas

Tollard
Royal

FONTMELL DOWN

GARSTON WOOD

Martin

Rockbourne
Roman Villa

Ashmore

Pentridge

Fontmell
Magna

LARMER TREE
GARDENS

Sixpenny
Handley

B3081

Farnham

Gussage
St Andrew

Chettle

Cranborne

B3078

Tarrant
Gunville

Gussage
St Michael

Wimborne
St Giles

Edmondsham

Tarrant
Hinton

Gussage
All Saints

A338

Pimperne

Tarrant
Launceston

KNOWLTON
CHURCH

Tarrant
Monkton

Witchampton

Horton

B3078

RINGWOOD

Tarrant
Rawston

Tarrant
Rushton

HOLT FOREST
&
HEATH

BLANDFORD
FORUM

THE TARRANT

Tarrant
Kyneston

Tarrant
Crawford

BADBURY RINGS

RIVER ALLEN

KINGSTON
LACY

B3082

WIMBORNE
MINSTER

RIVER STOUR

INNER CHASE

INTRODUCTION

I have often heard Cranborne Chase described as a secret landscape and perhaps that is the most appropriate description. It seems to be not too well known even among long-standing Dorset residents. I have quite regularly been asked just exactly where and what it is.

Perhaps the fact that it is not so well known has meant that its beauty has been preserved, making it one of Dorset's most atmospheric landscapes. Throughout the area open downland and rolling hills are punctuated with ancient woodland and coppice.

Driving south from Salisbury in the neighbouring county of Wiltshire, the traveller takes the A354 towards the famous Georgian town of Blandford Forum. Along the way the road passes through magnificent vistas, all sparsely populated. Occasionally there are distant views of woodland with glimpses of what appear to be ancient burial mounds. Nowhere do you see a signpost to Cranborne Chase, just the village of Cranborne signposted to the east of the A354 at a windy outcrop where the road is crossed by the B3081 linking Cranborne with such intriguing village names as Sixpenny Handley and Tollard Royal.

This area is almost the epicentre of the real Cranborne Chase, which lies both east and west of the main trunk road from Salisbury to Blandford Forum, hidden away from the passing traveller. Here the history of the Chase unfolds among the villages and woodland which have created this landscape over centuries.

The Chase is known throughout the world for its wealth of prehistoric sites, with 6,000-year-old 'long barrows', in essence Neolithic burial mounds. There is also the great Dorset Cursus, a Neolithic feature traversing the landscape for around 6 miles, together with a host of Bronze Age burial mounds more than 4,000 years old, and many other archaeological features yet to be discovered.

Thomas Hardy described this region of his beloved Dorset as 'the oldest wood in England'. Through these ancient woodlands, stretching across the chalk downland, royalty came to hunt deer and other game in the landscape which became known as 'the Chase'.

As a royal hunting preserve, the ancient laws of the Chase protected the animals and restricted the lives of the inhabitants. As a consequence, the landscape changed little until the mid-1800s when it was largely deforested, leaving much ancient woodland punctuated with farmsteads and agriculture.

However, what we see today is a landscape often described as austere but in reality is simply beautiful. It can be a silent and enchanting place which has developed an atmosphere from its past and history. Once a royal hunting preserve, fought over in both courts and land, today it is a place where wildlife and humanity live harmoniously together in an almost secret corner of Dorset.

It remains a landscape that provides a painting of its past with its open downland and wide expansive skies, dramatic escarpments and panoramic viewpoints. It even provides a sculptured view with its valleys and combes. Although it is a richly agricultural landscape, it remains peaceful and largely unspoilt with its own sense of remoteness.

The chequered history of Cranborne Chase has left its precise boundaries hard to define. Some ancient maps define the Chase as a narrow tract of land around 11 miles (18 km) long and approximately 2 miles (3 km) wide stretching from Gunville Down in the west to Bokerley Dyke in the east. However, the landscape surrounding this so called 'inner Chase' is too dramatic to be left out and I have allowed myself a little licence here in extending the boundaries somewhat in order to include towns, villages and areas all of which have had a direct link with the region. Thus, for the purposes of this book my boundaries have included villages and landscapes to the north towards Salisbury and the River Nadder south of the A303, with Shaftesbury in the west and Blandford Forum and Wimborne Minster in the south, following the north bank of the River Stour. Also included are locations just east of Cranborne, with some areas near Martin and Rockbourne defining an eastern boundary.

As a Dorset man I cannot help but refer to Cranborne Chase as being part of Dorset's landscape, but of course that is not strictly correct. The northern perimeter, including the River Nadder with its valley and villages, is very definitely in the southern edge of Wiltshire. Rockbourne's Roman villa, for example, also has its home in the neighbouring county of Hampshire, as indeed does the village of Martin and the nature reserve of Martin Down.

My sincere apologies to all those villages and locations who may have considered their proximity to the Chase warranted inclusion. The map featured at the beginning of the book has been based upon the Cranborne Chase Area of Outstanding Natural Beauty (AONB) boundary, but, regrettably, space prohibits widening the boundary beyond those of the historical inner and outer Chase.

In this portrait of an atmospheric landscape I can only hope that my photography and that of my long-term colleague and friend Roger Holman has given the reader an insight into the region, which has been so familiar to us both over the years.

This book is not intended to be an in-depth historical, archaeological or geographical textbook, as I am not remotely qualified to produce such a work. As a photographer and lover of landscape, my intention is that this book should be a personal portrait of an area which I find fascinating in its very nature and atmosphere. I have added elements of history that have moulded the Chase landscape and provided much of its unique character. For those requiring a more in-depth study of Cranborne Chase, I would recommend reading *Cranborne Chase* by Desmond Hawkins, the former BBC producer who founded the BBC Natural History Unit.

Perhaps the most relevant way to describe this location however is to revert to the master himself, Dorset writer Thomas Hardy, whose novels embrace the landscape so well, and Cranborne Chase in particular in *Tess of the D'Urbervilles*:

The soft azure landscape of the chase – a truly venerable tract of forest land, one of the few remaining woodlands in England of undoubted primaeval date, wherein Druidical mistletoe was still found on ancient oaks, and where enormous yew trees, not planted by the hand of man, grew as they had grown when they were pollarded for bows.

PHOTOGRAPHING THE LANDSCAPE OF CRANBORNE CHASE

The area of Cranborne Chase has always been a very familiar one for me. When I was a schoolboy it was a favourite region for cycling, and being relatively distant from my home in Wimborne, cycling on the Chase inevitably turned into an adventure.

As my interest in photography increased, the Chase again returned as a location to frequent in search of light on the landscape. As a result, I seem to have a considerable collection of images featuring the rolling chalk downs, the distinctive tree clump of Win Green and the ruins of Knowlton church.

Likewise, my friend and colleague Roger Holman, despite a tremendous photographic fascination for the Dorset coast, lived within the boundaries of the Chase for almost fifty years, overlooking the historical landscape surrounding Horton and its famous tower. Not surprisingly, with such outstanding landscapes on his doorstep, he too has amassed a significant collection of Chase landscapes.

After years of traversing the Chase, inevitably these days by car and throughout the seasons, it has always occurred to me how unchanging this landscape is. The views available to today's traveller are perhaps the same as those also familiar to the country folk of the region, from a time when they used the Ox Drove and the surrounding uplands to journey their cattle and sheep. Those travelling in horse-drawn carriages between London and Bath would have rested at the local hostelries, many of which are still in existence today, and witnessed the rolling downs and ancient burial sites, so characteristic of the Chase landscape, from their carriage windows.

With its history as a royal hunting ground, there are areas of estate and almost parkland appearance contrasting with the woodland and natural copse scattered throughout the scene which contrast with the chalk uplands and rolling hills. I have always considered there to be a certain atmosphere to the Chase landscape, no doubt resulting from its ancient past and a legacy from the lives lived and lost throughout its history. It can certainly be a landscape which speaks, and I have frequently felt a presence when alone on a windswept hill or in ancient woodland. Perhaps it is this 'atmosphere' which has attracted the creative minds of artists, writers and musicians who have made the Chase their home.

Just over two years ago I considered Cranborne Chase needed a closer look and exploration with a possible book in mind. With a camera, an Ordnance Survey map, an early copy of Michael Pitt Rivers' *Shell Guide* and perhaps the most detailed history of the Chase ever written (the aforementioned *Cranborne Chase* by the late Desmond Hawkins), I started researching and exploring what I thought was a familiar landscape. Inevitably, there were many surprises along the way and I soon found much more of the Chase than I had previously known.

Searching for that landscape image with a certain quality of light and in varying seasons usually results in a wealth of material from which to edit. In these conditions it can also be all too easy to capture scene upon scene of the rich open landscape. We have therefore tried to provide variety in our selection of images. The Chase has much to photograph in respect of rivers, woodland and nature reserves. There were also the villages and hamlets of the Chase to be captured and this perhaps is where things started to get just that little more challenging.

Inevitably, the villages of the Chase have had to provide for modern living. Although their inhabitants still live harmoniously with the surrounding countryside, it is unfortunate that images of modernisation should at times invade the scene. When trying to photograph the rural idyll one has to work around the mass parking of the motorcar, colourful wheelie bins, the inevitable 'For Sale' sign and of course perpetual building work or road repairs with their incandescent display of health and safety equipment.

Weather has also played its part. With the recent harsh and wet winters, a number of landscape trips were put on hold until the landscape had recovered from the ravages of storms and the floods had sufficiently subsided to permit access with our non-four-wheel drive modes of transport. There has also been the constant wait for clouds and skies to provide a more 'painterly' scene for the landscape. A white featureless sky is always something an artist can change with a brush; capturing a scene in camera of course becomes a little more difficult, unless one is tempted to deploy the facilities of Photoshop which, as something of a purist, personally I am less inclined to do.

Despite these 'intrusions', it has of course been a tremendously worthwhile project. We have perhaps photographed fewer sunrises than in *Landscapes of Dorset*, the first illustrated book Roger Holman and I photographed together back in 1991, a fact that has nothing to do with sunrises not being visible on Cranborne Chase. From a personal perspective it has probably more to do with the fact that one reaches a time in life when venturing into the cold and dark of a winter's morning, in search of an image which may not present itself, has to compete with those few extra hours of comfort!

One aspect of our photography which we have tried to maintain is that of timelessness. Most, if not all, of our images are devoid of people or wherever possible elements of modernisation. This is not by accident; it is a genuine endeavour to preserve the image of Cranborne Chase, and the naturally preserved landscape. We trust our images will have done justice to this end and will have preserved the scene for future enjoyment and fulfilment for generations to come.

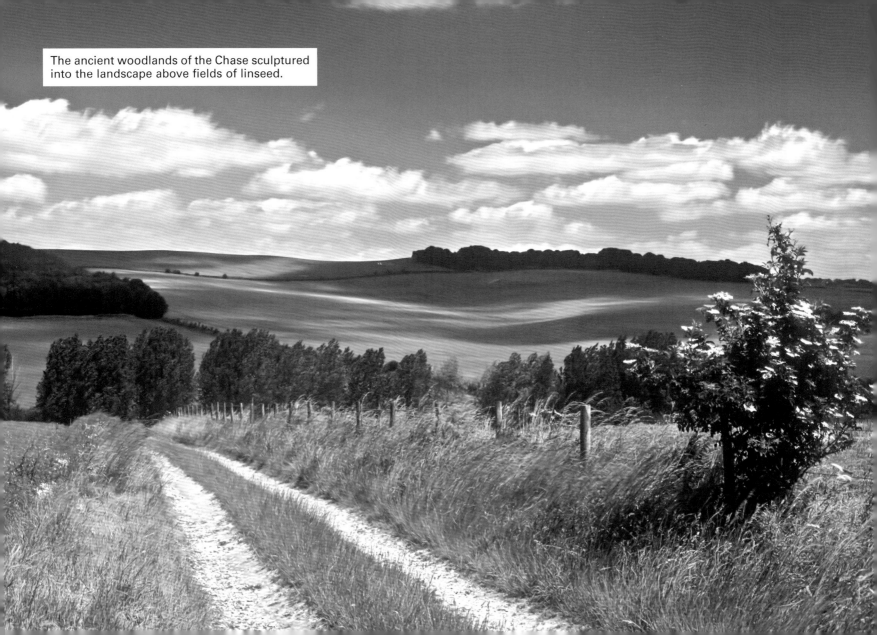

The ancient woodlands of the Chase sculptured into the landscape above fields of linseed.

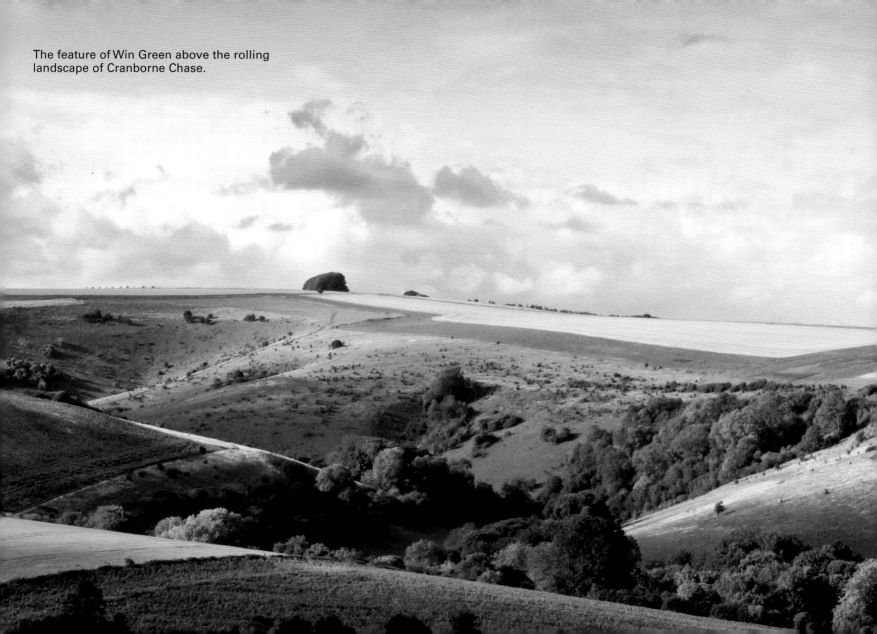

The feature of Win Green above the rolling landscape of Cranborne Chase.

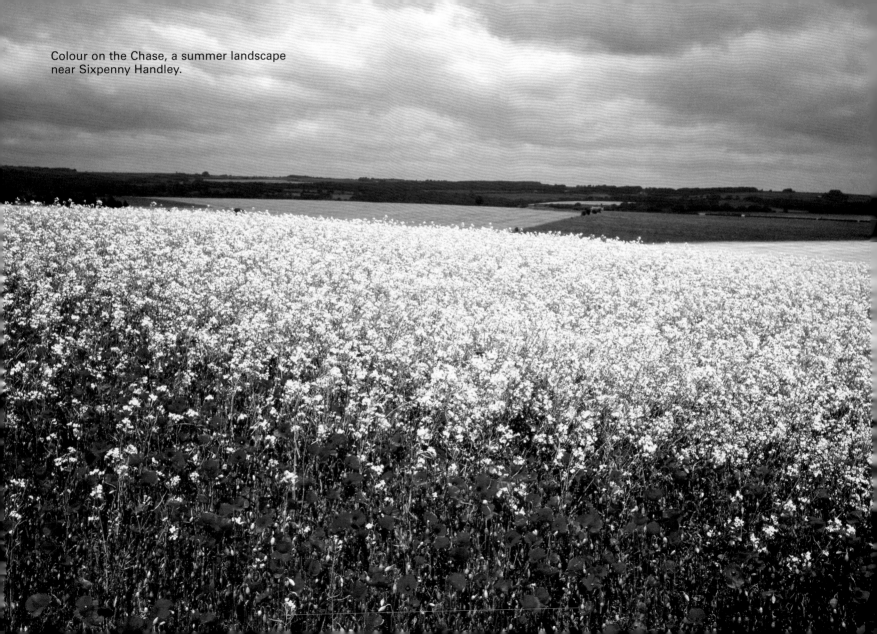

Colour on the Chase, a summer landscape
near Sixpenny Handley.

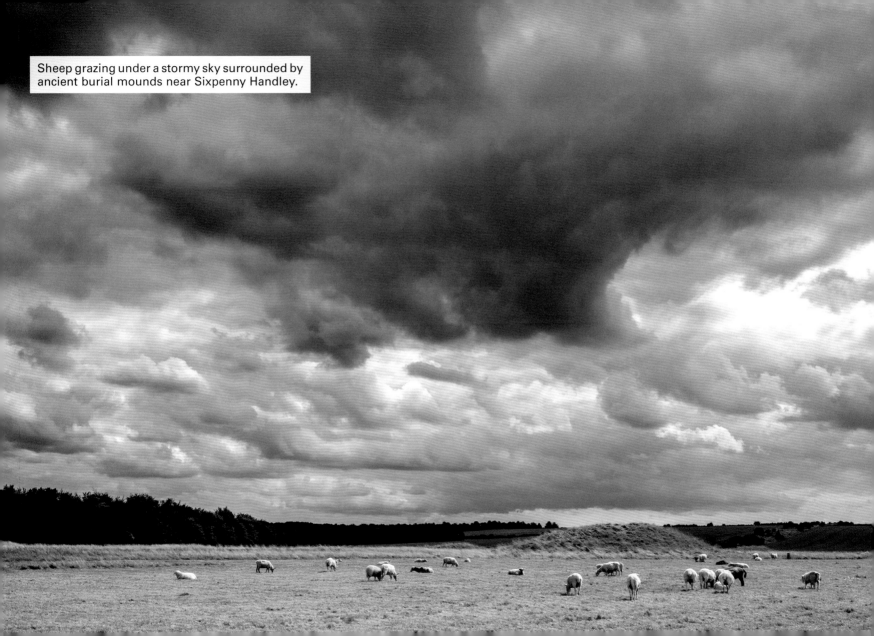

Sheep grazing under a stormy sky surrounded by ancient burial mounds near Sixpenny Handley.

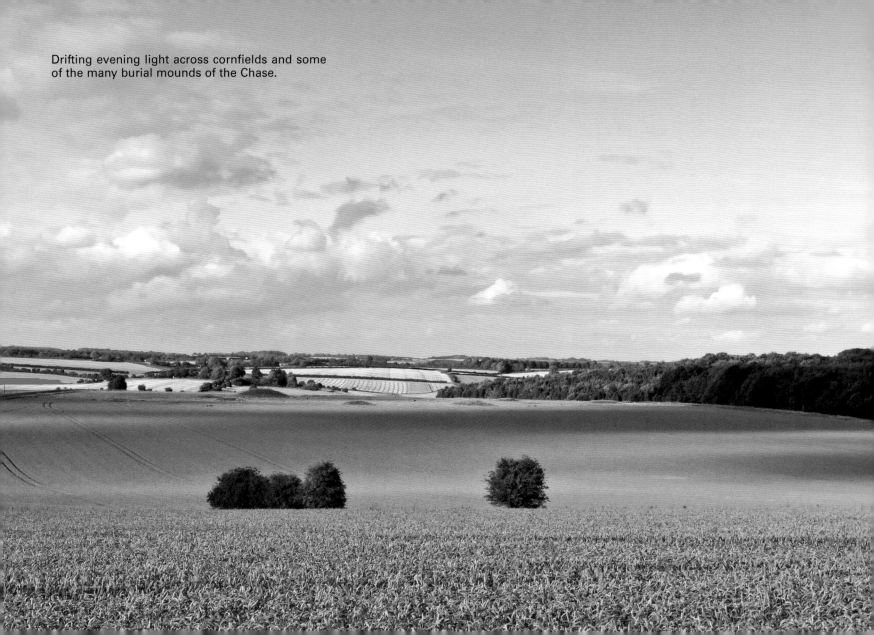

Drifting evening light across cornfields and some of the many burial mounds of the Chase.

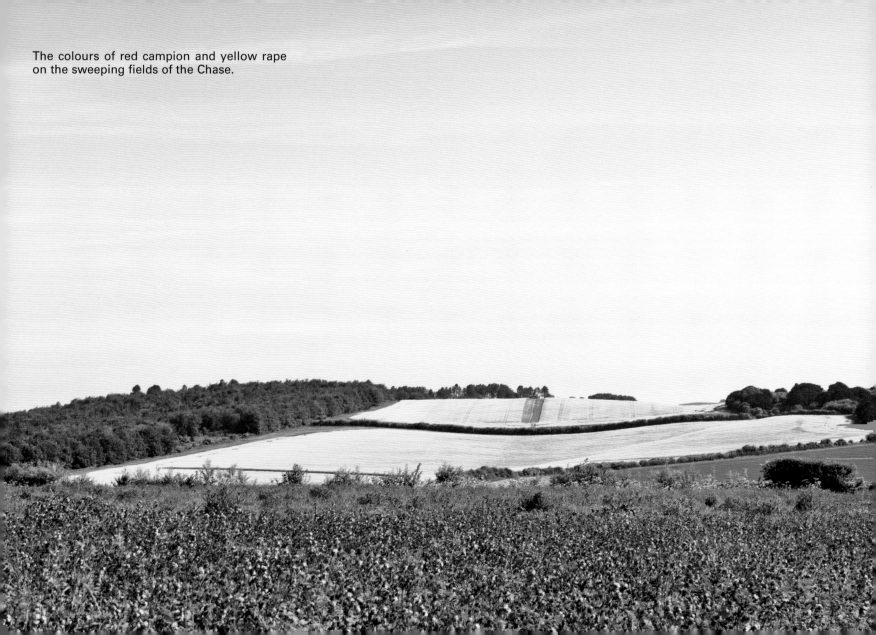

The colours of red campion and yellow rape
on the sweeping fields of the Chase.

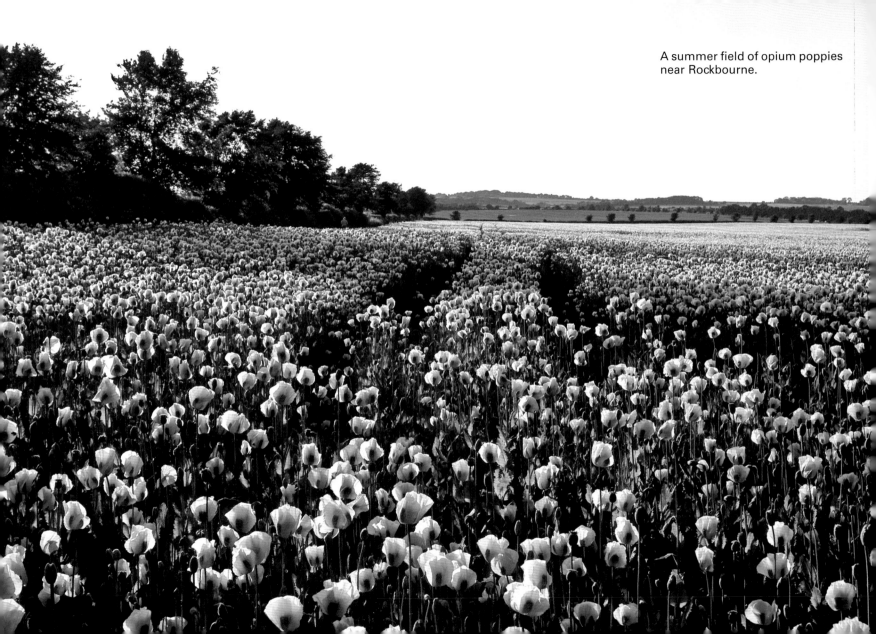

A summer field of opium poppies near Rockbourne.

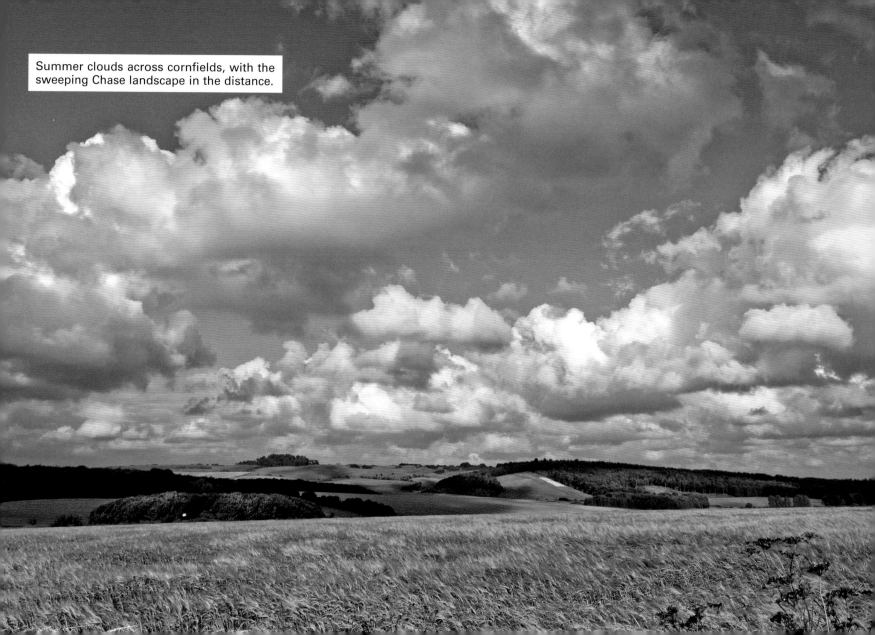

Summer clouds across cornfields, with the sweeping Chase landscape in the distance.

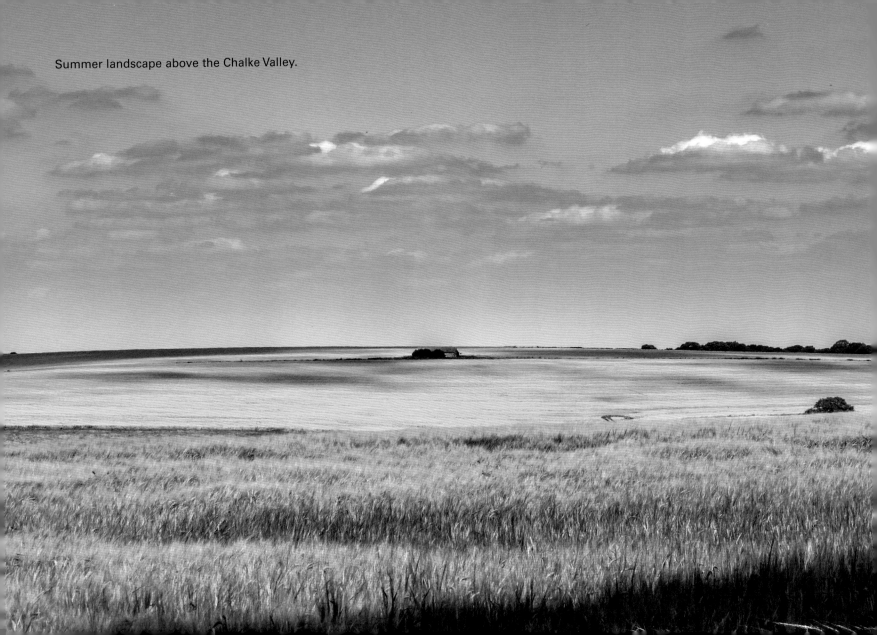

Summer landscape above the Chalke Valley.

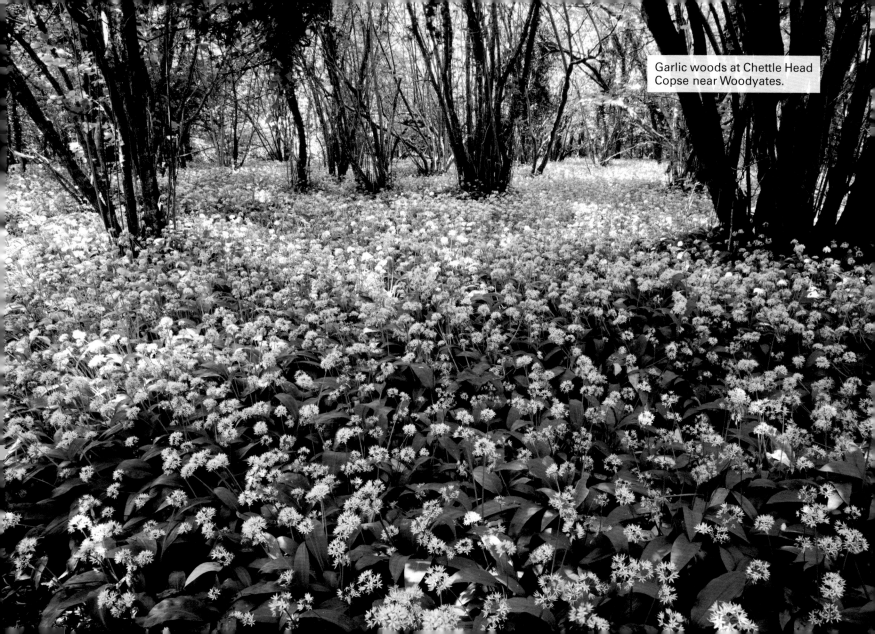

Garlic woods at Chettle Head Copse near Woodyates.

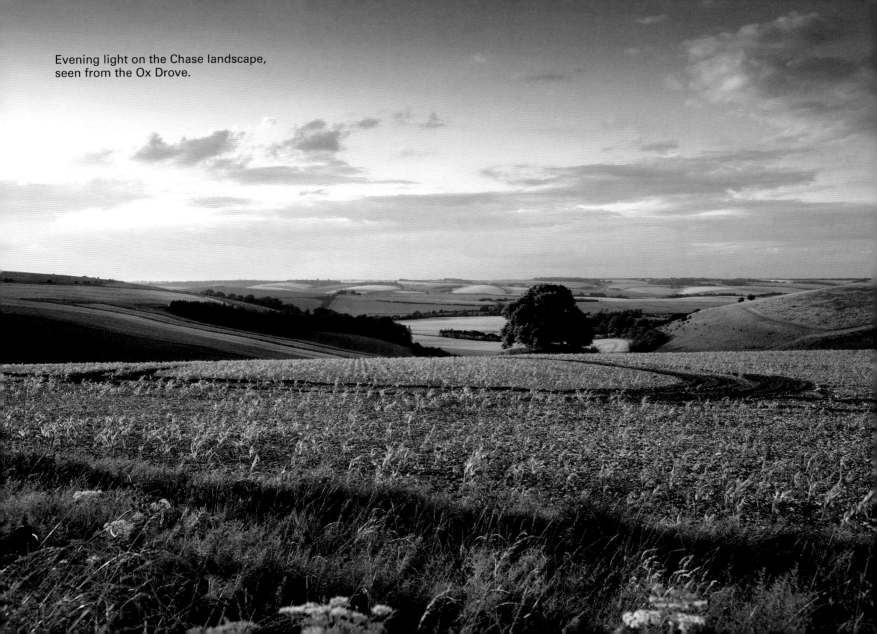

Evening light on the Chase landscape,
seen from the Ox Drove.

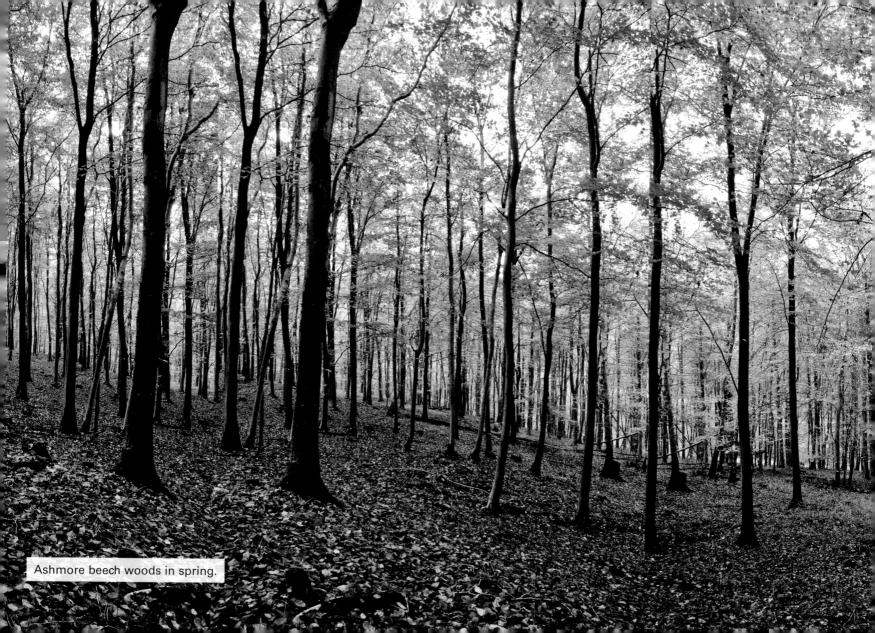

Ashmore beech woods in spring.

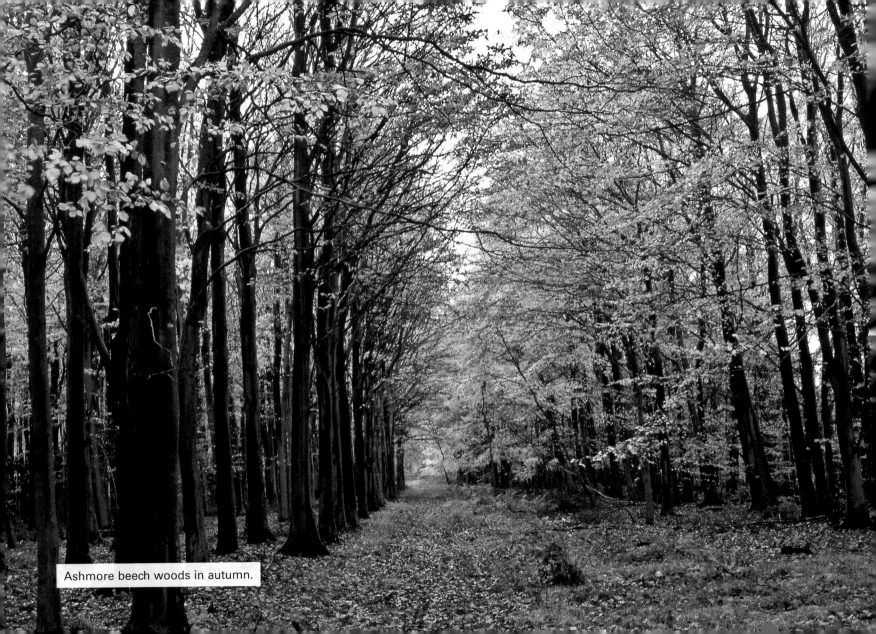

Ashmore beech woods in autumn.

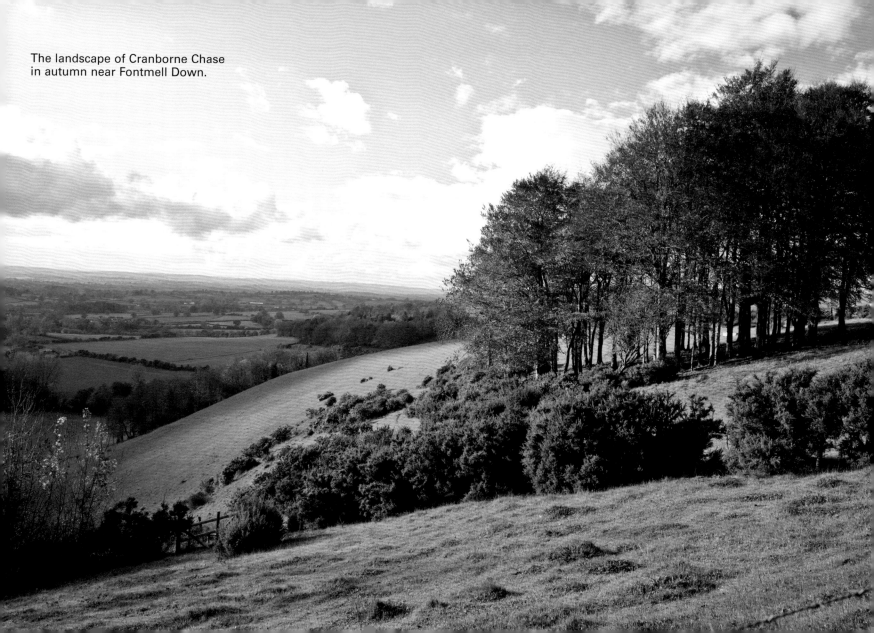

The landscape of Cranborne Chase in autumn near Fontmell Down.

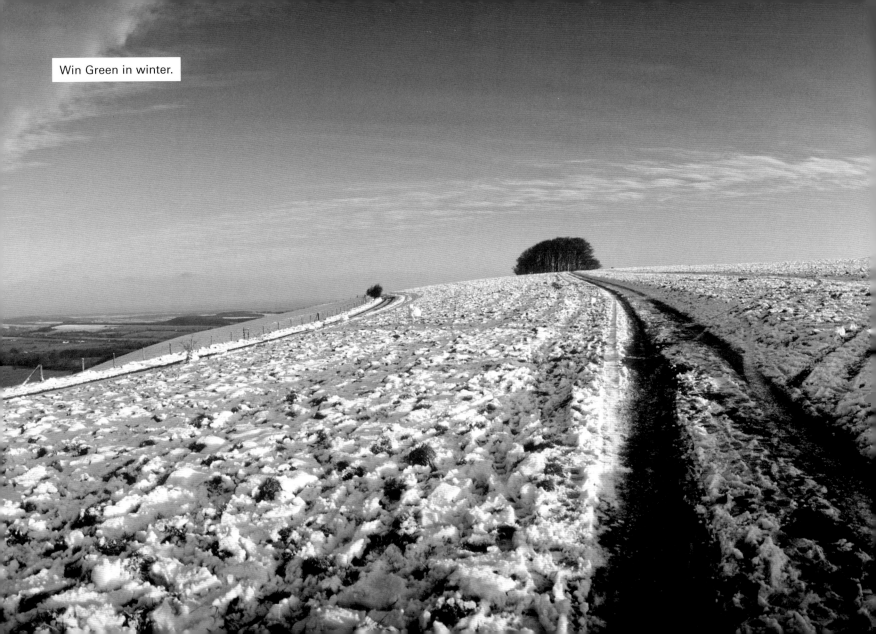

Win Green in winter.

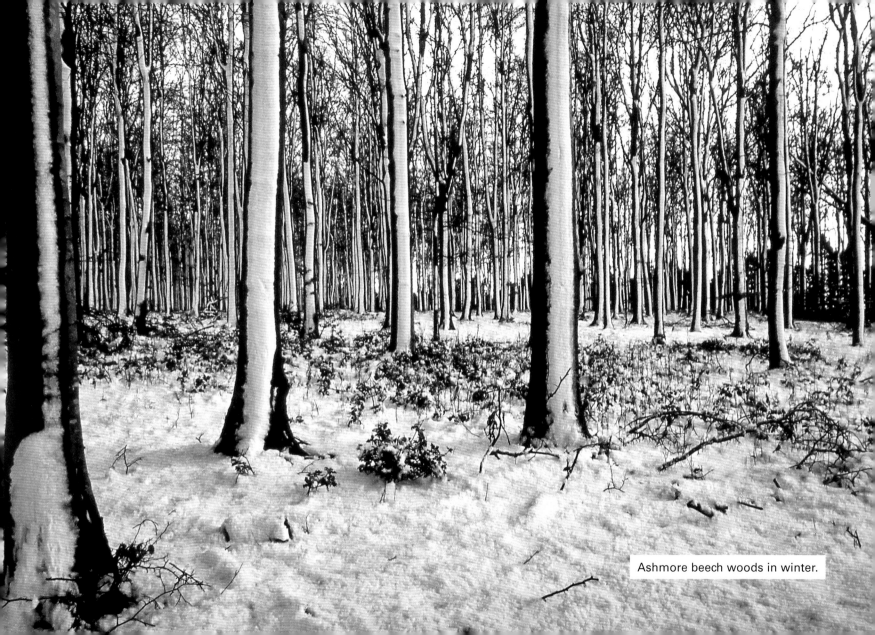

Ashmore beech woods in winter.

ACKLING DYKE

Ackling Dyke is the name of the Roman road which passed through the Chase from Sorbiodunum (Old Sarum) to Durnovaria (Dorchester) by way of the great hill fort of Badbury Rings near Wimborne Minster. It traverses the landscape roughly northeast to southwest and is one of the best known examples of a Roman road in the country. It remains banked in some areas to more than 6 feet high and makes a magnificent cross-country walk.

Walking this stretch of the Roman road can be an interesting and imaginative experience. It is not too difficult to visualise the legions, landowners and tradesmen who have travelled this way through a landscape of hills and valleys, over a chalky and stony turf with an occasional glimpse of bygone cultures.

In contrast, another dyke (Bokerley) further to the east was built around the fifth century as a defence for the inhabitants of Cranborne Chase against invasion from the northeast. It runs along the border of Dorset and Hampshire and through the naturally rich landscape of Martin Down.

Ackling Dyke on a summer evening.

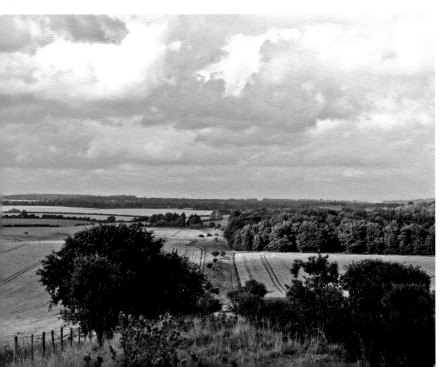

Ackling Dyke in winter.

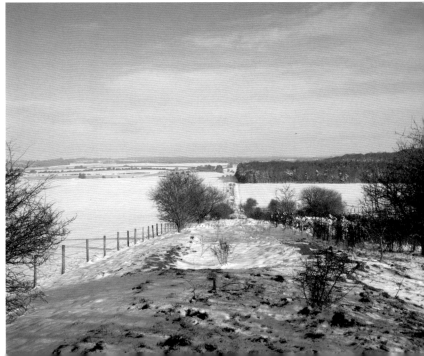

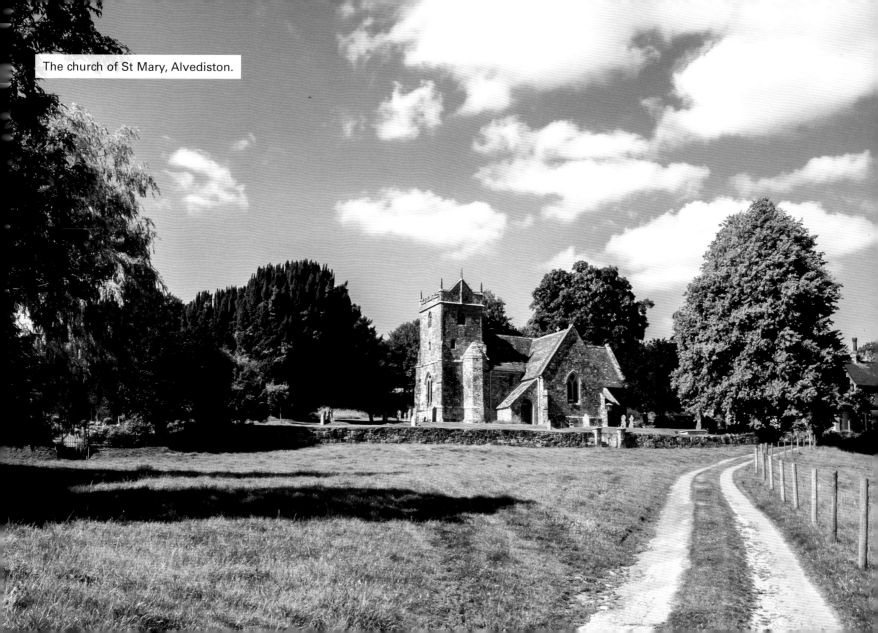

The church of St Mary, Alvediston.

ALVEDISTON

Alvediston is a small, attractive village with a fifteenth-century inn located in the Ebble Valley, southwest of Salisbury. The church of St Mary sits away from the village on a small hillside which slopes down to the River Ebble, providing a truly English landscape setting. Alvediston was the last home of PM Anthony Eden (1955–57), the 1st Earl of Avon, who is buried in the churchyard.

Below: Sheep grazing in the Ebble Valley at Alvediston.

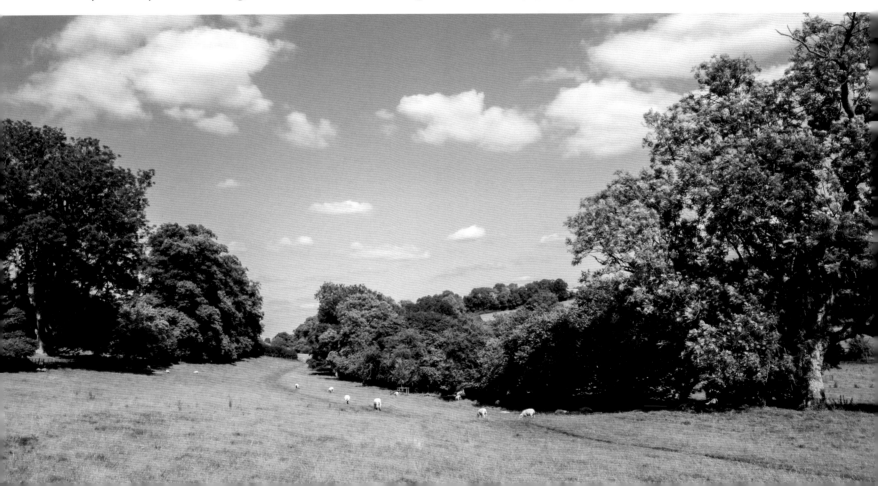

ASHMORE

Ashmore is the highest village in Dorset, set at some 700 feet above sea level with the surrounding landscape commanding far-reaching views into the neighbouring counties of Wiltshire and Hampshire. I remember as a boy cycling around here and being excited to take in glimpses of the distant Solent and chalk cliffs of the Isle of Wight. Unfortunately, in more recent times increasing tree lines appear to have limited this possibility.

The village is mentioned in the Domesday Book as 'Aisemere', seemingly derived from the Old English *aesc* and *mere*, meaning a 'pool where the ash tree grows'.

Ashmore village is approached down a lane at the end of which can be found a round, deep pond complete with ducks and village houses scattered around it which provides a setting reminiscent of an early English landscape painting.

It is suggested that the large pond in the centre of the village is from Roman times, possibly in existence when the Romans were building Ackling Dyke. At around 16 feet deep it rarely dries up, although there have been occasions when it has which allowed the farmers to retrieve the mud and spread it as a nutrient for their fields. At these times, a custom was to bake cakes as part of a feast held on the bed of the pond and around its circumference.

Ashmore's other custom performed around the village pond is the Filly Loo, a celebration of the longest day and held on the Friday nearest to 21 June when there is much dancing and merriment. A Green Man arrives in a procession and starts the evening of public dancing, followed by a torch-lit procession with six antlered Deer-men and four

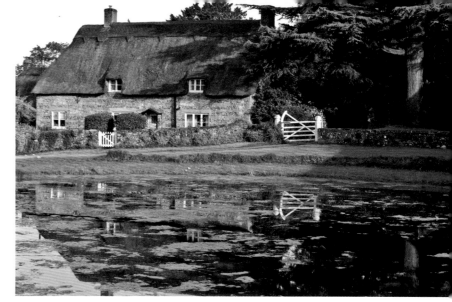

Above: Reflections in the village pond.

Below: Ashmore village and cottages.

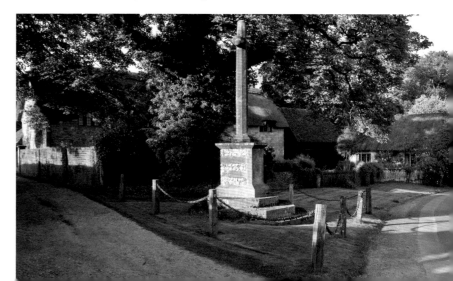

other costumed characters: Maid Marian, a Bowman, a Hobby Horse and a Fool. The procession is accompanied by a haunting melody which is very atmospheric. The celebration comes to an end with torches set in the ground around the pond and everyone holding hands for the last dance. The origin of the name 'Filly Loo' is unknown, but there is a suggestion that it originates from the name of a villager who introduced the custom, a Louis Rideout who was also known as Filbert Louis. Filbert is also another name for hazelnut and it has been said the Filly Loo was a custom to celebrate its harvesting.

A little-known piece of Ashmore's history concerns its association with the Society of Friends or Quakers. During the eighteenth century, John Eliot, a Quaker who opened a school in the village, became the Squire of Ashmore, but even earlier Ashmore had an association with the Society of Friends. Ashgrove Farm, just north of Ashmore, had been the home of William Fry since 1607 and was regularly used as a meeting house for members of the Society. Such meetings were of course illegal and frequently raided. William Fry was also prosecuted and imprisoned in 1660 for refusing to pay his tithes, but, despite his prosecution, later gave an area of his land to become a Quaker burial ground, as Quakers are not allowed internment in churches. William himself was buried there in 1708. Burials were recorded there between 1678 and 1775 and the area has been used in more recent times for both burials and the scattering of ashes. To preserve the right of way to the Quaker burial ground, it has now become a custom and tradition to organise a Quaker pilgrimage or procession to the site at the beginning of each decade and this is still done today.

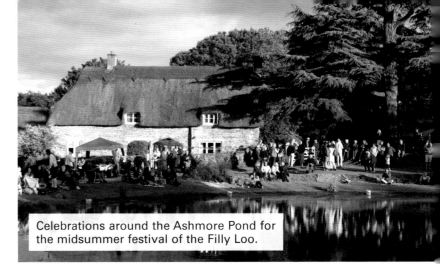

Celebrations around the Ashmore Pond for the midsummer festival of the Filly Loo.

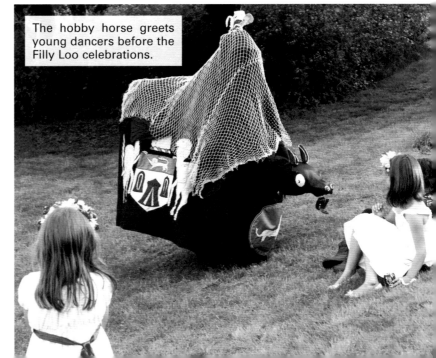

The hobby horse greets young dancers before the Filly Loo celebrations.

BADBURY RINGS AND KINGSTON LACY

Located just a short distance from Wimborne on the northern side of the road towards Blandford Forum is Badbury Rings, once an ancient hill fort and now a conservation area of recreation. It is situated overlooking the Stour Valley and lies on the southernmost edge of Cranborne Chase.

The ancient hill fort of Badbury Rings dates from the Iron Age, but is thought to have been built on a site occupied in a much earlier period, authenticated by the existence of Bronze Age round barrows still visible today.

The fort consists of three circular ditches protecting a central inner sanctum located at the very top of the hill in what is now woodland, where wattle and daub houses would once have been situated. There is evidence of entrances on the east and west sides. The ramparts, it is said, could have been as much as 40 feet high and even today provide a formidable climb in places. In the central woodland there is a dew pond, which may even have supplied the original inhabitants with water.

Badbury Rings is thought to have been the settlement of a Dorset tribe known as the Durotriges, which would almost certainly have been invaded by Romans, probably led by Vespasian under Emperor Claudius. A number of Roman roads have been found within the vicinity including links to Ackling Dyke and its route to Old Sarum and another coming up from the Roman port of Hamworthy on Poole harbour. All this provides a wonderful image of activity including trade, battles and pilgrimage throughout the area.

There is also a romantic notion that King Alfred met the Saxons here and this was his Mount Badon (or the Mons Badonicus)

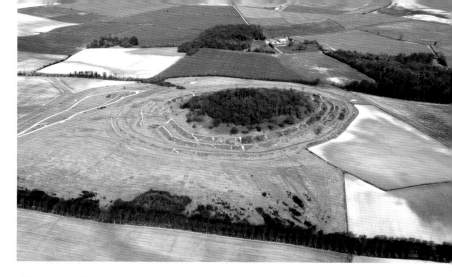

Above: Badbury Rings from the air photographed in 1981 for the National Trust audio-visual *The Greatest Gift*. The famous avenue of beech trees can be seen below the Rings and in the distance is the Roman road of Ackling Dyke.

Below: Badbury Rings and a herd of the distinctive Red Devon pedigree cattle.

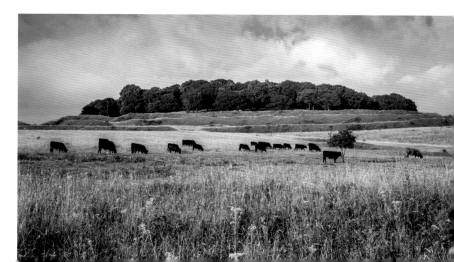

mentioned in the Anglo-Saxon Chronicle. Indeed, the chronicle does state the 'Black Heathen' were pressing up the Stour Valley to establish their 'Promised Land' to become the kingdom of the West Saxons. During these marauding times, Mount Badon was a particularly decisive battle and it is an interesting thought to consider it was here at Badbury.

This historical site is now under the management of the National Trust as part of the Kingston Lacy estate.

To the south of Badbury Rings runs the main Wimborne–Blandford road and the famous Beech Avenue. A remarkable sight in almost any season, providing a soft green canopy in summer and magnificent colours in autumn with atmosphere being added by early morning mists.

It is said the trees were planted by William John Bankes in 1835 in commemoration of his mother. There were 365 trees planted on one side of the newly opened turnpike road and 366 on the other. Over the years the ravages of winter storms and inevitable disease have reduced the numbers, but the National Trust's management programme continues to preserve this notable landmark stretching for more than 2 miles between Wimborne and Blandford.

The nearby Kingston Lacy House once formed part of the Royal Duchy of Lancaster, but in 1632 MP and lawyer Sir John Bankes purchased the estate and manor house together with Dorset's legendary Corfe Castle in the Isle of Purbeck. Being staunch Royalists, the Bankes family suffered greatly during the Civil War and not only lost their fortune but the family seat of Corfe Castle, which was remarkably defended against two severe Parliamentarian attacks by Sir John's wife, Dame Mary Bankes, following his death in 1644. The castle was eventually captured and destroyed in 1646, resulting in the famous landmark ruins we see today.

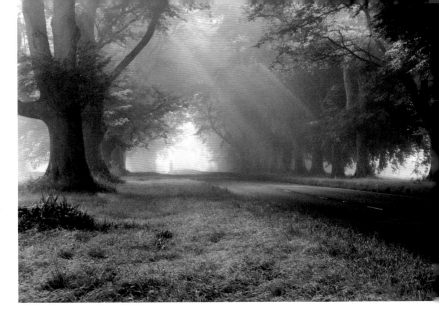

Above: The famous avenue of trees at Badbury Rings, seen here enhanced by early morning rays of light.

Below: The dew pond amid the trees within Badbury Rings.

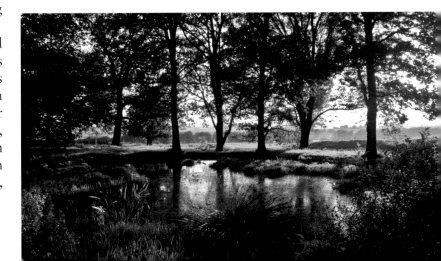

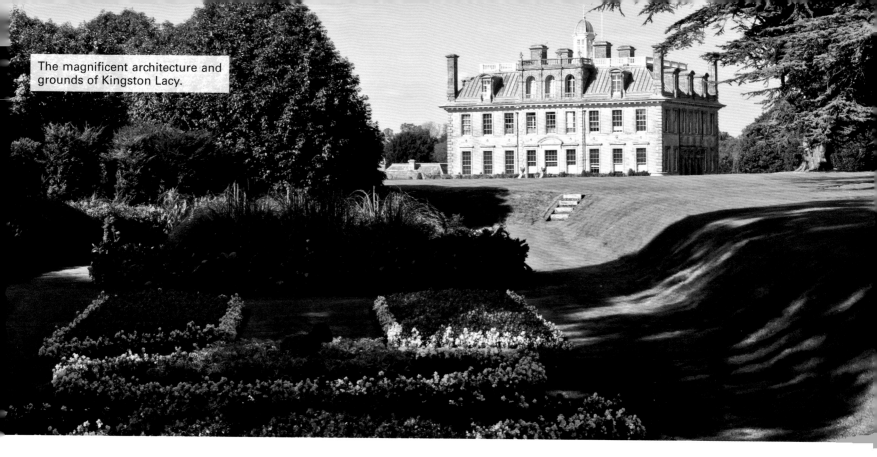

The magnificent architecture and grounds of Kingston Lacy.

In 1663, Sir Ralph Bankes, also an MP and lawyer like his father, managed to secure the estate and commissioned the building of a new family home, naming it Kingston Hall. Unfortunately, Sir Ralph also fell into debt and on his death it became necessary for his son, William John Bankes, to let the family home to raise much needed funds. Fortunately, some years later, the Bankes family were able once more to return to their ancestral home and managed to stay there for the next 300 years. During this time the house was renamed Kingston Lacy and underwent a considerable transformation, resulting in the imposing architectural masterpiece by Sir Charles Barry which can be visited today.

The surrounding estate and gardens remain a living monument to the Bankes family, whose estate was left to the National Trust in 1981.

At this time Roger Holman and I were privileged to photograph the entire estate for the National Trust, producing an audio-visual documentary entitled *The Greatest Gift*, which was shown to the first visitors to Kingston Lacy House. Indeed, at that time it was the greatest gift the National Trust had ever been bequeathed.

BERWICK ST JOHN

Berwick St John lies at the head of the Ebble Valley approximately 5 miles east of Shaftesbury. Behind the village, White Sheet Hill marks the elevated pre-turnpike route and Ridgeway from Salisbury. Nearby Winklebury Hill, which dominates the village, has an Iron Age hill fort on its summit, from which views span across to the neighbouring counties.

Being located within the Cranborne Chase and West Wiltshire Downs Area of Outstanding Natural Beauty, the village is surrounded by rolling chalk grasslands, ancient woodlands, chalk escarpments and river valleys, but things could so easily have changed when Berwick St John almost became the Paddington or Waterloo of Cranborne Chase. In 1875 there was a proposal from an Arthur Pain for a horse-drawn or light railway stretching 15 miles from Salisbury via Coombe Bissett and along the Ebble Valley to terminate at Berwick St John. It was to be named the Chalk Valley Railway. However, Mr Pain found little support for his proposals and the railway never saw the light of day.

Interestingly, the great bell of Berwick St John's church has a story to tell. In 1746 the rector, John Gane, required in his will that at eight o'clock every night between 10 September

Berwick St John's church.

Berwick St John.

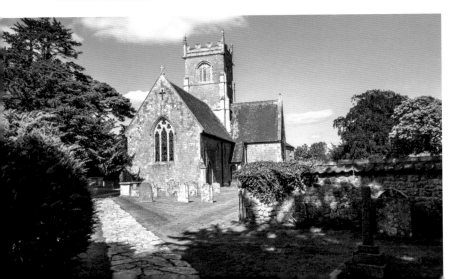

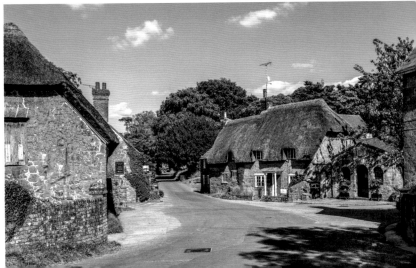

and 10 March the bell should be rung for fifteen minutes to guide any lost travellers on the high chalk downs of the Chase to safety. On the high uplands at night, with few milestones or markers to assist, lost travellers became a common occurrence in Gane's day. This practice carried on until the 1960s when the village could no longer find a willing bell-ringer to undertake the nightly task.

BLANDFORD FORUM

Blandford, or more precisely Blandford Forum, was all but destroyed by a serious fire in 1731 from which only a few buildings have survived. This in a way was Blandford's unique offer to Dorset, being rebuilt in the Georgian style by the talented brothers William and John Bastard.

Today, façade after façade of Georgian architecture decorate this Stour-side town. Seemingly, since the 1700s, Blandford has been a garrison town and continues to be so as the home of the Royal School of Signals and the Royal Signals Museum.

Here Gen. Wolfe is said to have reviewed the troops before sailing for Quebec, before meeting victory and death on the Heights of Abraham. More poignantly perhaps for a town set amid such beautiful Dorset landscape, the poet Rupert Brooke wrote his famous lines when stationed at Blandford as part of the Royal Naval Division (RND).

> If I should die, think only this of me:
> That there's some corner of a foreign field
> That is forever England…

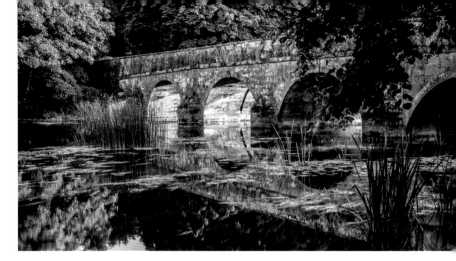

Above: The River Stour at Blandford Forum captured in evening light.

Below: Blandford's corn exchange captured as a reflection on a day of festivities.

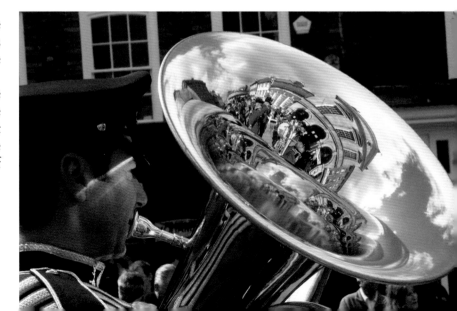

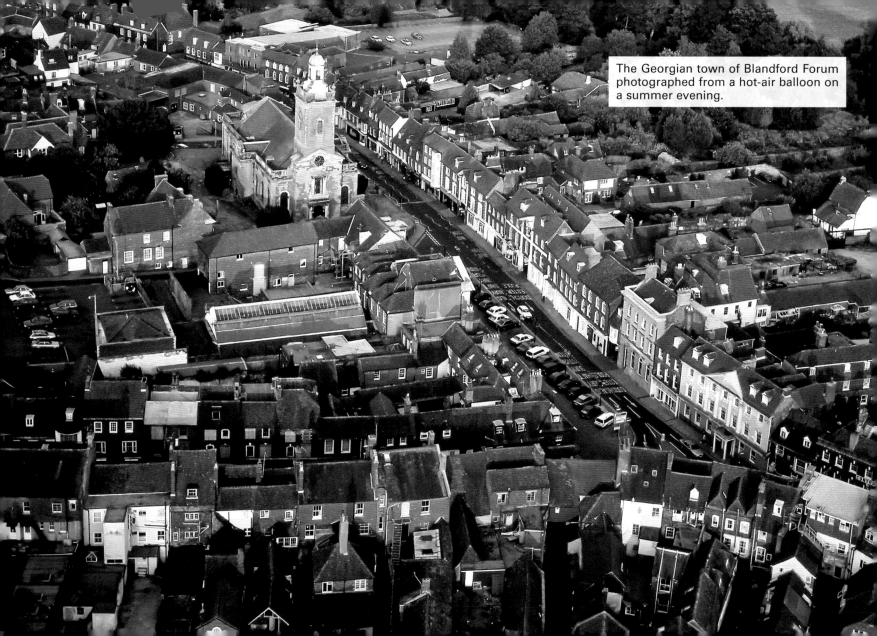

The Georgian town of Blandford Forum photographed from a hot-air balloon on a summer evening.

BOWERCHALKE

The village lines the road which drops down from the chalk escarpment. Here in this attractive settlement, the River Chalke rises in the village and later joins the River Ebble at Broadchalke before flowing into the Avon south of Salisbury.

This beautiful valley lies between the two main ridge walks: the Ox Drove from Win Green and the Salisbury Way, once used by stagecoaches en route from London to Exeter via Salisbury and Shaftesbury. On either of these high ridges it is still possible to experience the same views as ancient travellers would have seen many hundreds of years ago.

Nobel Prize winner and novelist William Golding, author of *Lord of the Flies*, once lived in a cottage on the banks of the River Chalke and is buried in the churchyard of the thirteenth-century church of the Holy Trinity.

Folds in the landscape above Bowerchalke with a distinctive barn on the horizon.

Dappled sunlight on fields above Bowerchalke.

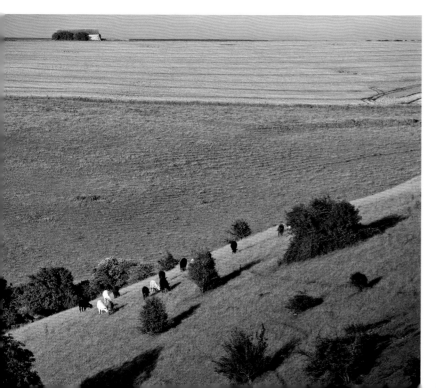

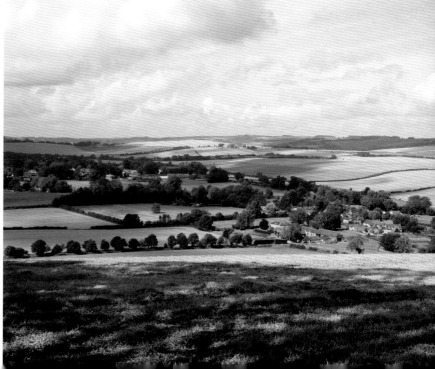

BROADCHALKE

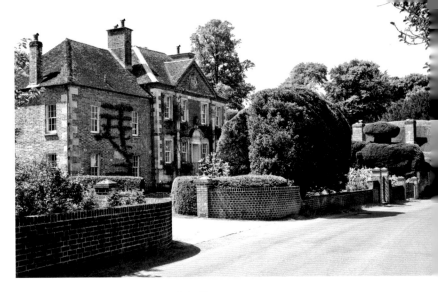

Above: Reddish House, Broadchalke.

Below: Broadchalke's All Saints church.

Broadchalke is one of the larger villages in the Ebble Valley and is never far from the sound of running water with the River Chalke flowing through it. All Saints church dates from around the thirteenth century with a fifteenth-century tower. Within the village are some grand properties with a mixture of thatch, stone and flint.

Over the years many notable people have lived in this village. Photographer Cecil Beaton bought Reddish House in 1947 and here immersed himself in village life, allowing his beautiful landscaped gardens to be used for village fêtes. The eighteenth-century house with origins going back to the sixteenth century was extensively renovated and extended in Beaton's time. It is said that he found the upper floor had been originally equipped as an area for illegal cockfighting, with cages still in existence through which the fighting was viewed. Beaton used these cages in which to store the costumes used in the set designs for *My Fair Lady*. The eighteenth-century house saw many famous visitors in Cecil Beaton's time, notably Greta Garbo, David Hockney and Princess Margaret.

In his writings, Beaton remarks how in just six weeks Greta Garbo fell in love with Broadchalke, the seclusion of Reddish House and the country food. He said there was something about the rural life that Garbo loved and she took to Wiltshire as if that was where she belonged.

Cecil Beaton remained at the house until his death in 1980 and is buried in the churchyard of All Saints church.

Other notable residents of Reddish House have been Wimborne-born rock legend and guitarist Robert Fripp and his singer and actress wife, Toyah Willcox. They moved to Broadchalke from their other Chase home in Witchampton, just north of Wimborne, in December 1987 and lived there until July 1999.

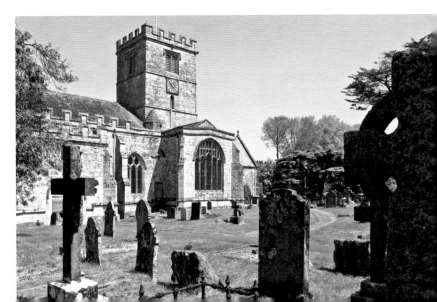

Since 1993, Broadchalke was also the home of novelist Sir Terry Pratchett. He became a familiar figure, walking around the surrounding landscape which he did so much to protect. Sir Terry died at his home in March 2015.

CHETTLE

The small estate village of Chettle lies on the west side of the A354 north of Blandford Forum and has been in the ownership of one family for more than 150 years. This area is full of earthworks and antiquities, with Chettle Down providing important finds from the past. Identified as 'Ceotel' in the 1086 Domesday Book, the name 'Chettle' refers to the location of the village; the Old English for 'kettle' means a deep valley surrounded by hills.

Chettle House (a private residence and not open to the public) is a Queen Anne manor house in the English Baroque style. It was built around 1710 by Thomas Archer for the MP and ranger of Cranborne Chase, George Chafin. It is reputed to have taken twenty-five years to build using materials from the surrounding area. It features rounded corners which are a unique design and specific to the style of Thomas Archer.

Chafin was renowned for his hunting on the Chase and his protection of its hunting rights. This frequently led him into local feuds and on one occasion he was challenged to a duel. Even his grandson continued the Chafin's turbulent history when he shot a woman on his first outing with a shotgun.

Edward Castleman, a Wimborne solicitor and the man who introduced the first railway to Dorset, bought the house in 1846 and considerably restored it. He also renovated the nave, chancel

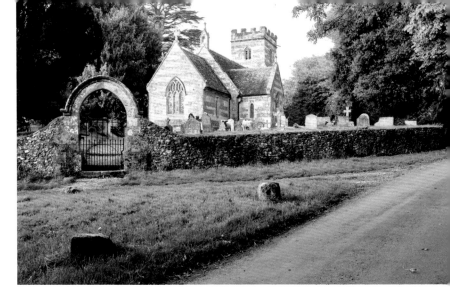

Above: St Mary's church, Chettle. Sheep can be seen grazing in the churchyard in this early autumnal setting.

Below: Morning mists across the landscape at Chettle.

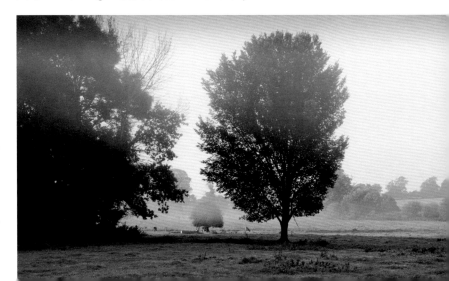

and vestry of the adjoining St Mary's church. With its sixteenth-century west tower, it is set within the grounds of Chettle House and provides a most suitable backdrop to the landscape.

COMPTON DOWN AND COMPTON ABBAS

In my view, one of the most dramatic drives in Dorset is from the top of Spreadeagle Hill out of Melbury Abbas towards Fontmell Down and Blandford. The views are quite breathtaking on both sides of the road and it is best to stop in one of the few parking areas to take in the splendour. Compton Down falls towards the west from the heights of Spreadeagle Hill and in certain lighting conditions can provide some amazing landscapes as the light transforms the folds and lines of the Down.

Nestling beneath the Down is the village or hamlet of Compton Abbas, which can be accessed on the lower Blandford to Shaftesbury road (A350). It is sheltered in the lee of Compton Down, Melbury Down and Fontmell Down, all high escarpments of Cranborne Chase, and looks out over Hardy's 'Vale of Little Dairies', the Blackmore Vale.

The name 'Compton' is derived from the Saxon *cumb-ton*, meaning a village in a narrow valley and the 'Abbas' refers to the abbey at Shaftesbury and the abbess who owned the land on which the village is located.

There are two churches in Compton Abbas, but one, a fifteenth-century example, is now only a ruined tower and is located in what Ordnance Survey maps describe as East Compton. The main church of St Mary was built nearer the centre of the village in 1866 using some materials from the old church.

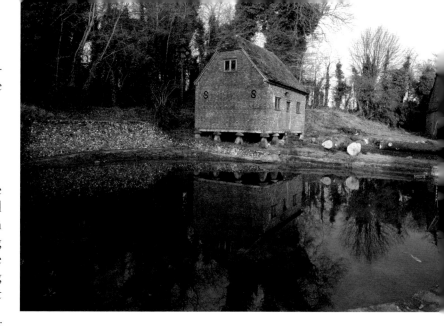

A rural scene at Chettle with a granary on saddle stones reflected in the village duck pond.

Returning to the heights above the village we find Compton Abbas Airfield located at 803 feet above sea level. It is without question one of the most picturesque grass airfields in the country. From its location on the western edge of Cranborne Chase the views span well into Wiltshire and the Blackmore Vale. No scheduled flights are available, of course, but it certainly has a reputation for being one of the friendliest flying clubs and provides a welcome to everyone, whether you have a yearning to learn to fly, to experience a flight in a vintage Tiger Moth or are simply a casual visitor taking in the views and watching the aircraft from the comfort of the restaurant.

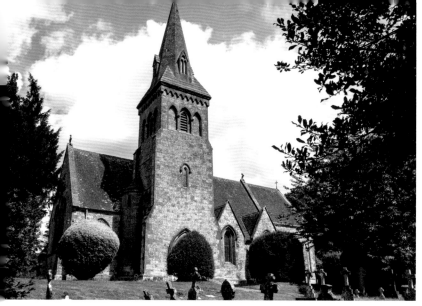

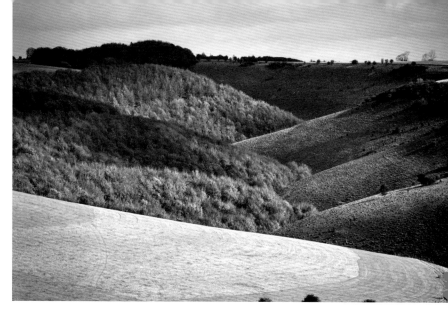

Above: The church of St Mary, Compton Abbas.

Below: Flying at Compton Abbas airfield on a summer evening.

Above: Evening light across the folds of Compton Down.

Below: Grounded – Compton Abbas airfield in winter.

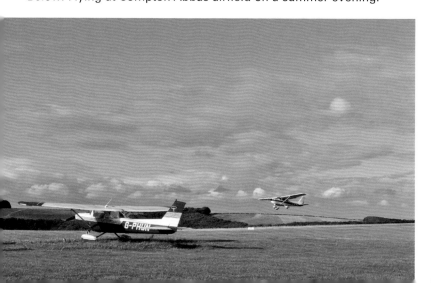

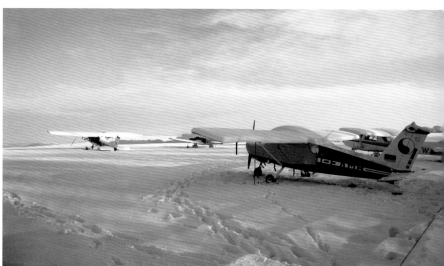

CRANBORNE

Dorset writer Monica Hutchings in her book *Inside Dorset* describes Cranborne as 'an attractive place, old, casual, quiet, not consciously a "beauty spot" but full of its own character'. To me it has always seemed a most suitable description, with its setting amid thickly wooded hills with a wide main street and attractive byways.

The River Crane, from which Cranborne gets its name, flows down from Pentridge and through the grounds of Cranborne Manor, no doubt assisting with the value of Cranborne as an early Saxon settlement. Further downstream, a little to the southeast of the village, are the remains of a Norman fortification at Castle Hill.

There was originally an abbey here established around 980 and the manor of Cranborne belonged to the Queen at the time of the Domesday Book. It was inherited by her son, William Rufus, but later became part of Tewkesbury abbey. The original manor was built as a royal hunting lodge for King John in the twelfth century when Cranborne Chase was a royal hunting ground, as it remained until the seventeenth century.

The Chase Courts were held here and their specific type of local justice administered, with the dungeons now part of the kitchen. Both James I and Charles I frequently stayed at Cranborne during hunting expeditions.

Robert Cecil, the 1st Earl of Salisbury, acquired the manor from James I in 1604.

Cranborne Manor is one of the most interesting houses in Dorset. Largely built of grey stone complete with mullioned windows, porticoes of twisted columns and tall red-brick chimneys, it is surrounded by formal gardens left much as they were by the designer Montagu Jennings and the plant collector John Tradescant. The house is not open to the public but can be glimpsed from the road along its tree-flanked drive. Robert Cecil's descendants still retain Cranborne Manor today.

Church Street, Cranborne.

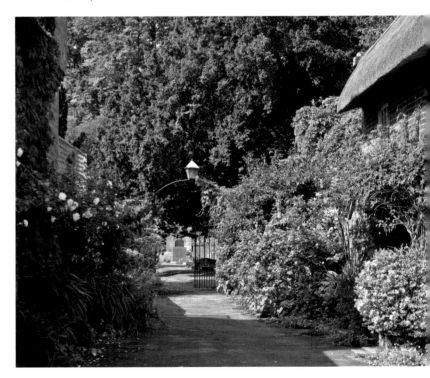

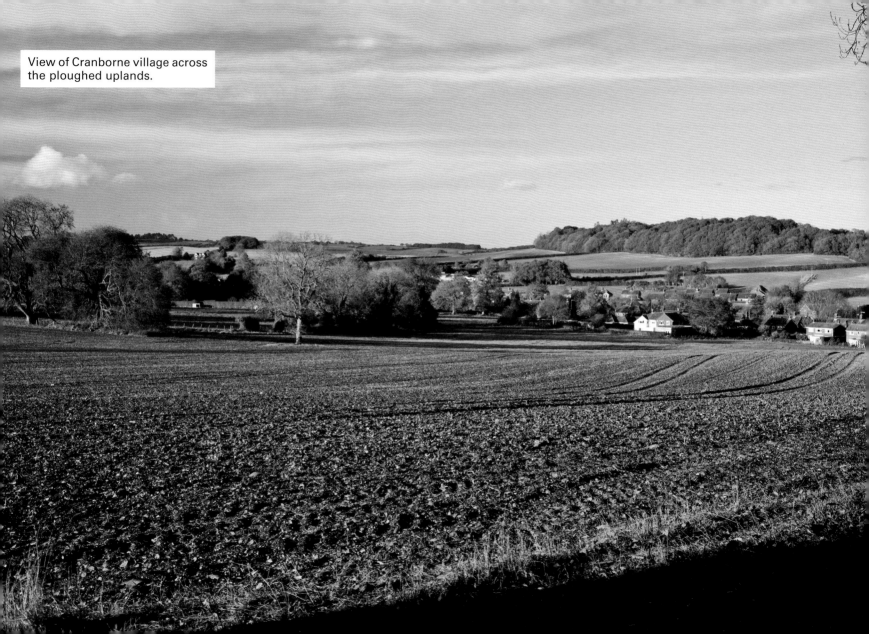

View of Cranborne village across the ploughed uplands.

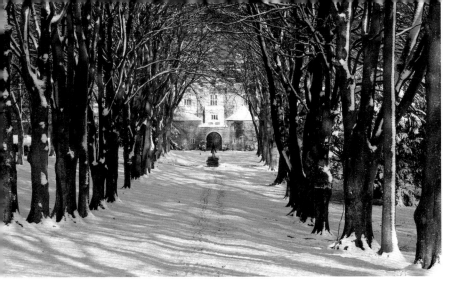

Above: View of Cranborne Manor in winter.

Below: Remains of a Norman fortification near Cranborne at Castle Hill.

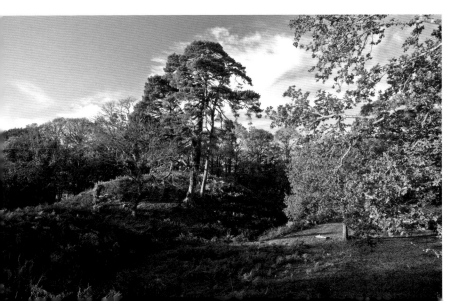

CRANBORNE'S ANCIENT TECHNOLOGY CENTRE

With the history of Cranborne Chase featuring prominently in archaeology it is perhaps not surprising to come across a unique venture located just outside the village of Cranborne, with its own history steeped in archaeology and ancient crafts.

The Ancient Technology Centre was formed just over twenty-five years ago as a school project headed by Jake Keen, a teacher at Cranborne Middle School. The initial project was based on the building of an Iron Age roundhouse using only locally available natural materials gathered by the schoolchildren from reed beds and woodlands. From the very start it was the intention that the building should also be constructed by the school children and within a year the roundhouse was completed, marking the start of a venture which continues this same ethos today.

Many of the traditional skills used at the centre have been introduced by Reg Miles, a true Dorset craftsman who still works on the site and has a passion for handing down his knowledge to young people. Now managed by Luke Winter, an experimental archaeologist, the centre has six full-sized reconstructions of ancient buildings including a Viking longhouse used as a residential building for educational courses.

With its team of staff and volunteers, Cranborne's Ancient Technology Centre has developed a unique method of hands-on learning for young people involving the exploration of their surroundings, environment and history. The result is a lasting piece of history developed by children in their own time and by their own hands.

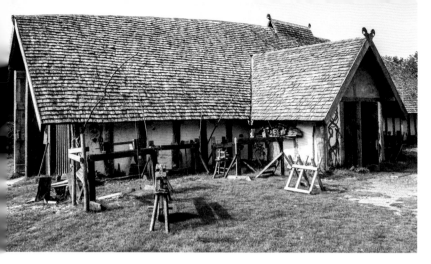

Above: The Viking longhouse – the largest reconstruction to date.

Below: The original roundhouse has been renovated after twenty-six years of use.

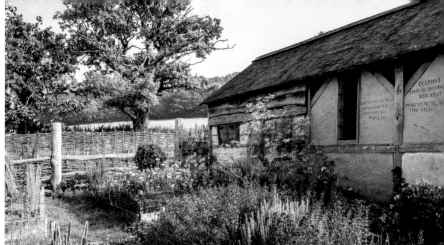

Above: The Roman forge – the walls have been painted with Latin graffiti from Pompeii describing the exploits of various gladiators. The garden is designed for growing herbs and plants introduced during the Roman period.

Below: Interior of the earthhouse, which is used for education purposes and for atmospheric evening storytelling events.

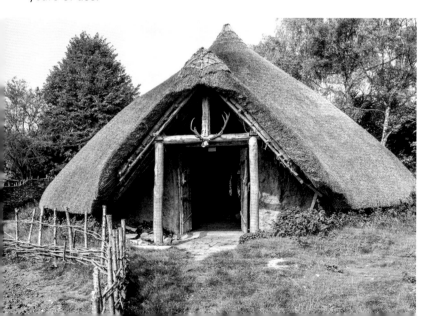

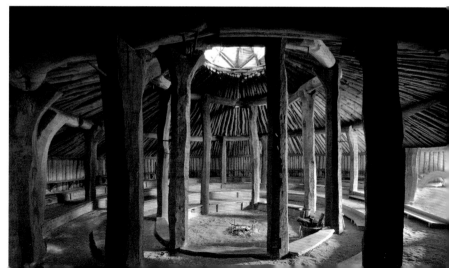

EBBESBOURNE WAKE

The Chalke valley in which the charming village of Ebbesbourne Wake resides is part of the Cranborne Chase and West Wiltshire Downs AONB.

The name possibly derives from the Wakes family who held the manor in the time of King John, and of course the 'bourne' is simply the valley and River Ebble. However, it was named as Eblesborne in the Domesday Book, and although there is no traceable proof as to why the coat of arms of Hereward the Wake can be found on the fifteenth-century church tower of St John the Baptist, it is somewhat coincidental.

It is a delightful area punctuated with thatched cottages and occasional glimpses of the river, remaining always shaded by the neighbouring mature woodland.

However, for just a few days each year this charming corner of Cranborne Chase becomes home to an international community who are welcomed to the annual Chalke Valley History Festival. This is the largest literary festival devoted to history and attracts many specialist historians and celebrities with exhibits, talks and displays both on the ground and in the air, all celebrating our heritage and past.

Shady Ebbesbourne Wake.

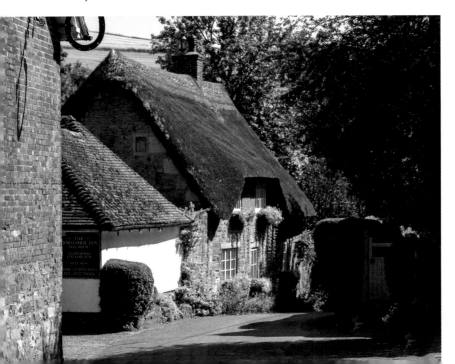

A plaque on this wall in the village provides memories of past village life.

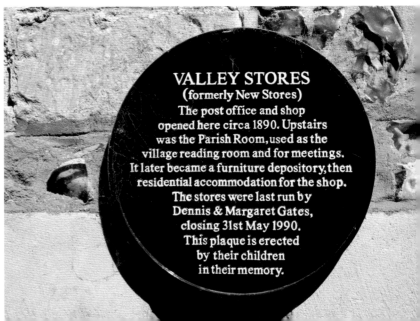

VALLEY STORES
(formerly New Stores)
The post office and shop opened here circa 1890. Upstairs was the Parish Room, used as the village reading room and for meetings. It later became a furniture depository, then residential accommodation for the shop. The stores were last run by Dennis & Margaret Gates, closing 31st May 1990. This plaque is erected by their children in their memory.

EDMONDSHAM

Edmondsham lies on the southernmost edge of the Chase surrounded by ancient woodland. The Church of St Nicholas dates from the twelfth century and is approached through a lych-gate and stands next to the dominant Tudor manor, built in 1589, which features gently rounded gables. This property has remained within the ownership of the same family since the sixteenth century.

The manor's attractive grounds and gardens are regularly open to the public. Included are special displays of spring bulbs, a walled garden and organic vegetable gardening. Here also are sloping lawns said to have originally been the site of medieval cockfighting.

Halloween pumpkin display in Edmondsham village.

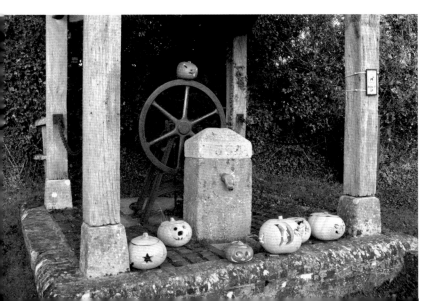

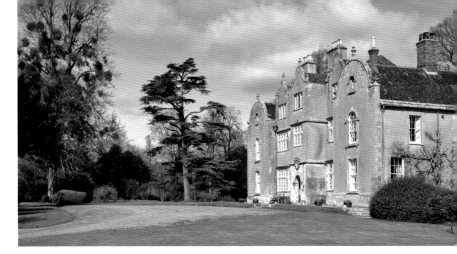

Above: Edmondsham Manor House with adjacent trees covered in mistletoe, quite characteristic of the area.

Below: The cock-fighting pit at Edmondsham House.

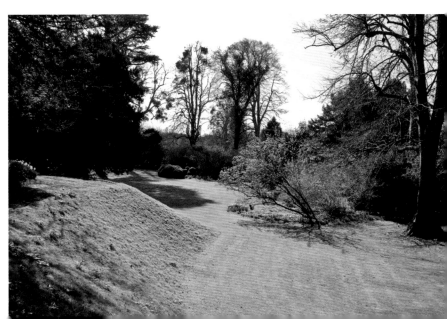

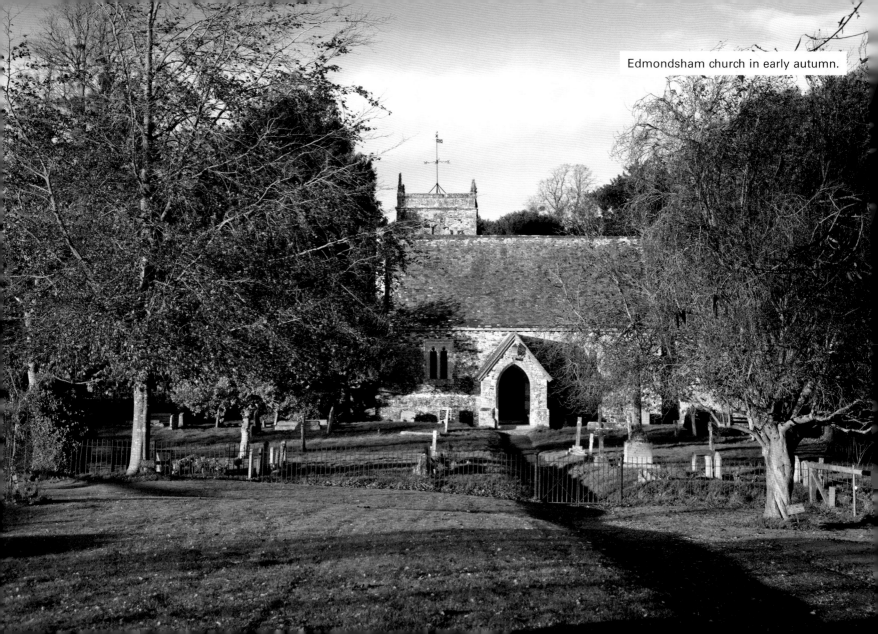

Edmondsham church in early autumn.

FARNHAM

A secluded village with thatched cottages, many of which have been built end on to the road with many having individual wells, as in fact does the village.

The Museum Inn is a hostelry dating from the seventeenth century and was built by Gen. Augustus Lane Fox Pitt Rivers for the use of visitors to his nearby museum. Pitt Rivers was a wealthy landowner in the area who also restored King John's Hunting Lodge at Tollard Royal and established the Larmer Tree Gardens. The once famous Pitt Rivers Museum contained many antiquities, artefacts and items of archaeological importance acquired by the General on his travels and more importantly from his many excavations on Cranborne Chase. The museum is now a private residence and the items have been relocated, with the local collections housed in Salisbury Museum.

Farnham cottages with the characteristic well in the front garden.

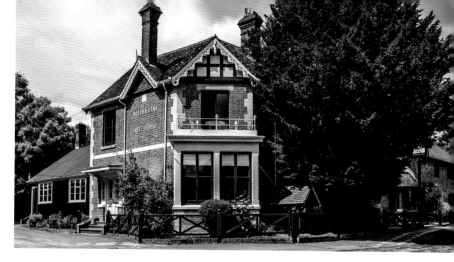

Above: The Museum Inn at Farnham.

Below: Farnham village well.

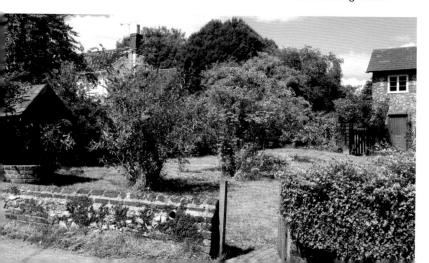

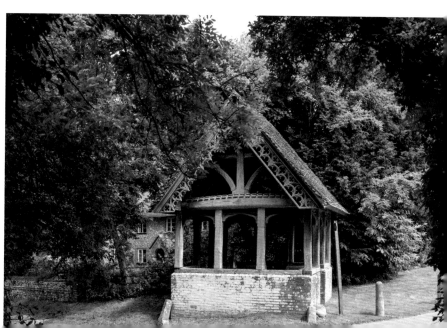

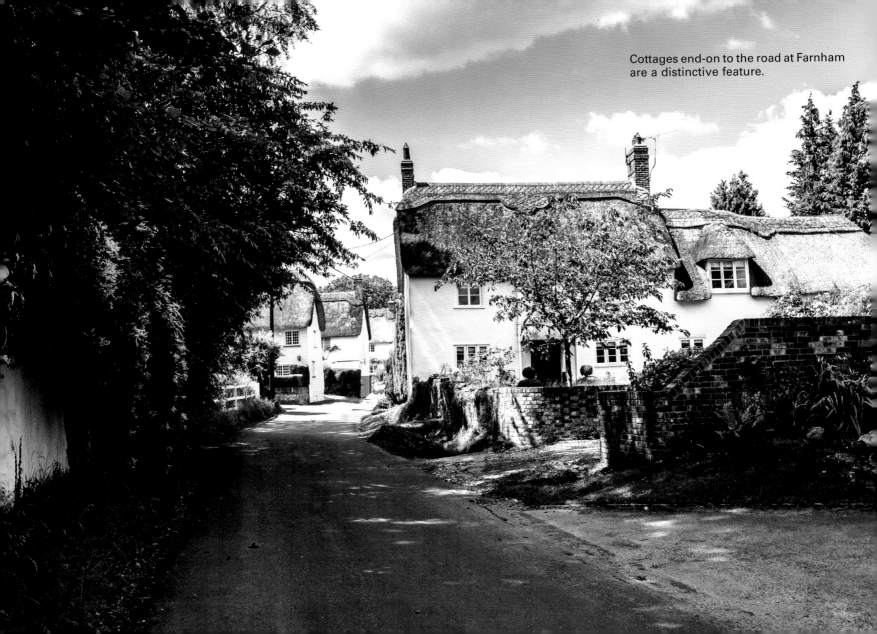

Cottages end-on to the road at Farnham
are a distinctive feature.

FIFIELD BAVANT

Fifield Bavant contains the church of St Martin, the smallest parish church in Wiltshire. It is also thought to be the second smallest in England in regular use. Measuring just 35 feet by 14 feet, it was erected in the thirteenth century. The flint and stone walls are thought to be almost entirely original. The turret was added in the early twentieth century.

The village itself is also the smallest in Wiltshire, with the foundations of the original medieval village still visible in the nearby valley.

In 2005, Fifield Bavant was a location chosen for the film *Pride and Prejudice*. The location fee was used towards the restoration of the church.

The small church of St Martin nestles in the landscape surrounding Fifield Bavant.

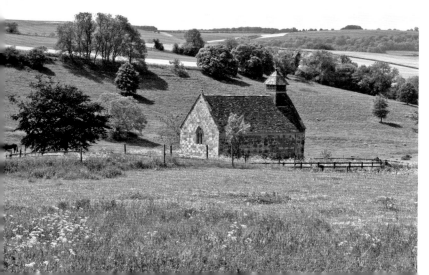

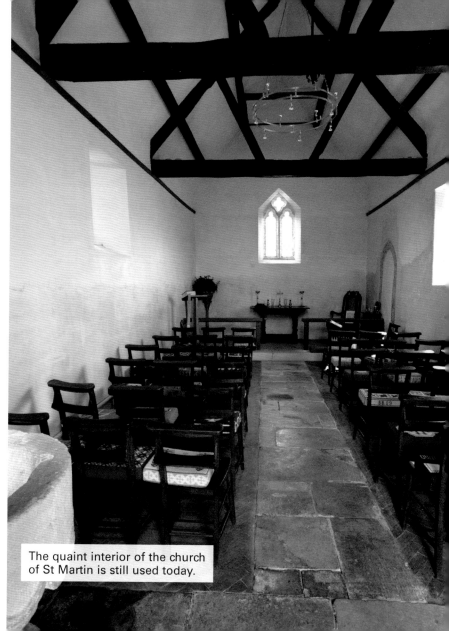

The quaint interior of the church of St Martin is still used today.

FONTMELL DOWN

At the top of Spreadeagle Hill on the road between Shaftesbury and Blandford the traveller will gasp in awe at the scene both left and right of the road. To the left is the downland of Cranborne Chase and the familiar clump of trees at Win Green. To the right however is Fontmell Down, probably one of the most memorable landscapes in Dorset.

Fontmell Down is a steeply sloping nature reserve with far-reaching views into the Blackmore Vale. In spring and summer the lower slopes are carpeted with rare wild flowers that thrive in calcareous soil, including orchids and early gentian. This is also a splendid habitat for many species of butterfly.

Such is the importance of this site, that it has been designated a European Status of Special Area of Conservation. Part of Fontmell Down is owned by the National Trust and the remainder by the Dorset Wildlife Trust, who provide the management of the whole area to maintain this wonderful downland wildlife habitat. The National Trust made their purchase in 1977 through public subscription and dedicated it to the memory of Dorset's Thomas Hardy in order to protect the landscape which inspired his novels.

It is thought this chalk downland site was created by man in the Bronze Age during deforestation. The sloping terrain made ploughing impossible so natural grazing of sheep and other animals provided the rich grassland which continues to provide the rare natural chalk grassland we see today.

In mid-October 2009 a field above Fontmell Down provided a rare sight of fields of poppies flowering as though it was midsummer. Apparently the soil structure, which had lain dormant for years, was disturbed by ploughing and in the mild weather the latent poppy seeds flourished and provided a magnificent display.

Looking west from Fontmell Down in winter towards Blackmore Vale.

Fontmell Down in autumn.

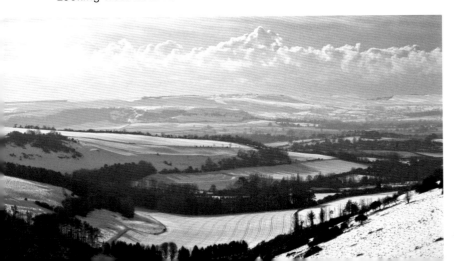

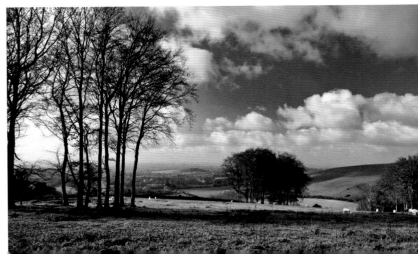

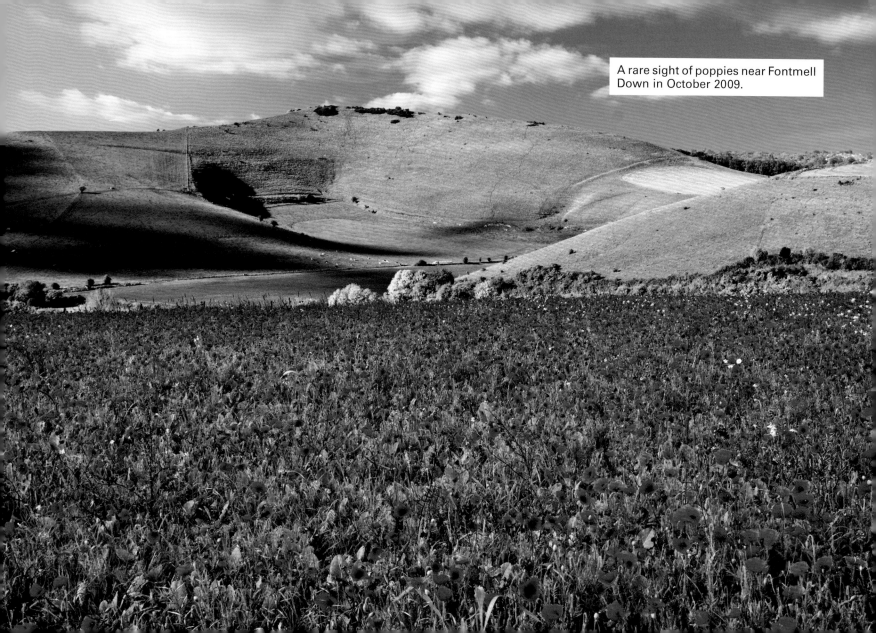

A rare sight of poppies near Fontmell Down in October 2009.

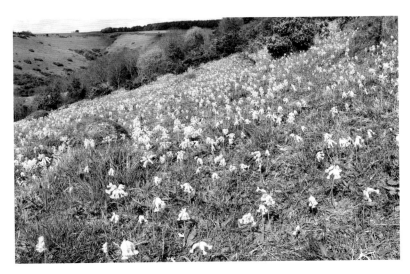

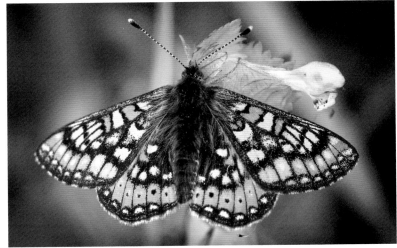

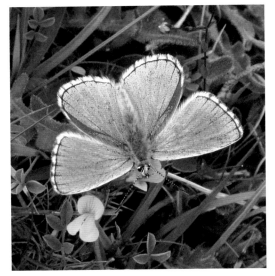

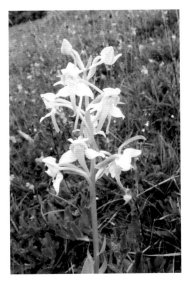

Above: Spring cowslips (*Primula veris*) on Fontmell Down. (*Courtesy of Tony Bates*)

Left: Adonis Blue butterfly (*Polyommatus bellargus*) – a native of the chalk down. (*Courtesy of Tony Bates*)

Above: Marsh Fritillary butterfly (*Euphydryas aurinia*). (*Courtesy of Tony Bates*)

Left: Greater butterfly orchid (*Platanthera chlorantha*). (*Courtesy of Tony Bates*)

FONTMELL MAGNA

The village of Fontmell Magna lies on the western fringe of Cranborne Chase along the lower road between Shaftesbury and Blandford Forum. Together with the neighbouring villages of Compton Abbas, Sutton Waldron and Iwerne Minster it sits comfortably between Cranborne Chase and Thomas Hardy's famous 'Vale of Little Dairies', the Blackmore Vale.

It is an attractive, typically Dorset village with a number of charming thatched cottages, some in traditional flint and brick, and once belonged to the Abbess of Shaftesbury until the Dissolution of the Monasteries in 1539.

At one time the village had three mills, all of them water mills powered by the Fontmell Brook. These mills provided a source of income to the village for many years, supporting the local cloth, corn, timber and forging trades. Today the springs still rise from the chalk uplands of Cranborne Chase.

World renowned orchestral conductor Sir John Eliot Gardiner was born in the village, the son of Rolf Gardiner (1902–71), an English rural revivalist who focused on the return of folk dance styles including Morris dancing and sword dancing. He also pioneered significant interest in organic farming.

Set above the centre of the village, much of the present church of St Andrew was rebuilt in 1862/63 by Sir Richard Glyn, then lord of the manor and owner of much of the village.

A quiet corner of Fontmell Magna alongside the millstream.

The village of Fontmell Magna overlooked by the downland of Cranborne Chase, viewed from the church grounds. In the centre can be seen one of the village's former mills.

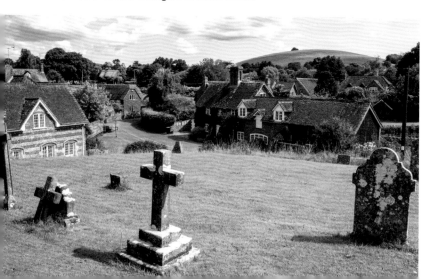

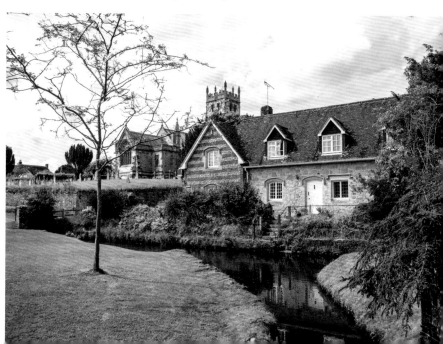

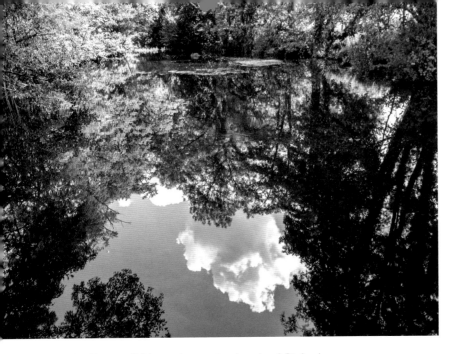

Left: Reflections in Collyer's Brook at Fontmell Magna. This delightful pond is maintained by the Dorset Wildlife Trust after being donated in 2005. It is fed by no fewer than ten chalk springs over a distance of 1,148 feet from the site.

Right: Fontmell Magna's ornate church of St Andrew.

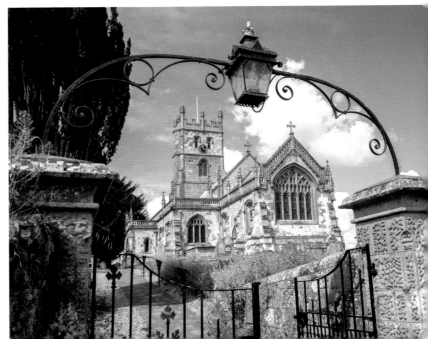

THE GUSSAGES

These villages are just on the outside of the inner or ancient Chase, each with their selection of farm buildings and homes of mixed flint and brick. The three villages follow the valley of the Gussage Stream, which runs for approximately 5 miles before joining the River Allen. It is thought the name 'Gussage' derives from the Old English *gysic*, which means gushing stream, or *gwysch*, a watercourse that dries up for part of the year.

Gussage All Saints lies closest to the former medieval villages of Bowerswain and Brockington, but history has revealed that the site is much older, as there was once an Iron Age chariot factory here which became extinct around AD 80.

It is Gussage St Andrew however that has a secret in its little church of St Andrew. Hidden behind the farmhouse is what might on first inspection be considered to be another barn, but no, it is a simple and ancient church.

Harvest time near Gussage All Saints.

Records indicate this small chapel of St Andrew was originally a wooden chapel built by King Alfred as part of Shaftesbury abbey. When the wooden structure burned down it was replaced by the present chapel in the twelfth century. The chapel was dedicated to St Andrew the fisherman.

During the 1950s, traces of thirteenth-century wall paintings were discovered here when restoration work was being carried out and were described as being of national importance. They are believed to have been painted by travelling craftsmen in the twelfth century with figures added in the thirteenth century followed by text in the seventeenth century. The travelling artists generally painted scriptures as few people could read and there were no English translations of the Bible.

The paintings were restored in 1966 and in 2012 were stabilised, conserving them for future generations.

An old farm cart at rest, photographed beside the road some years ago on a frosty morning in the Gussages and believed to have since been restored.

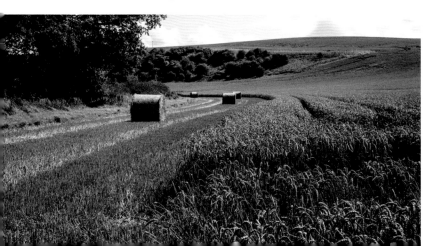

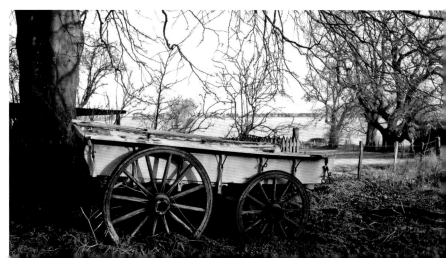

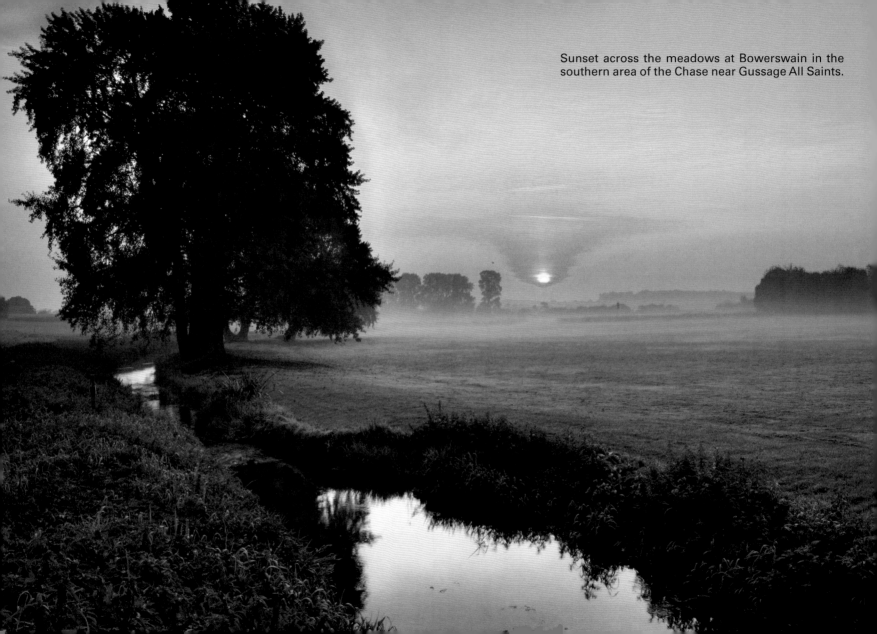

Sunset across the meadows at Bowerswain in the southern area of the Chase near Gussage All Saints.

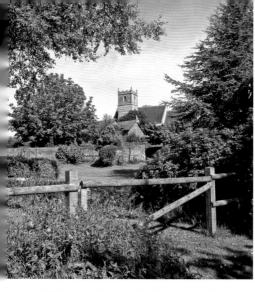

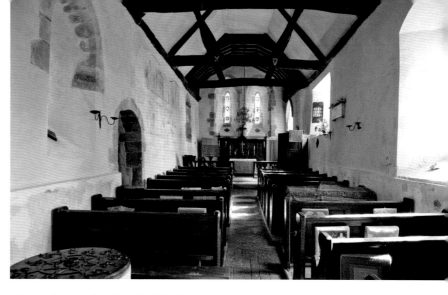

Left: Gussage All Saints.

Below: The chapel of St Andrew.

Above: Inside the chapel of St Andrew.

Below: The rare, ancient wall paintings.

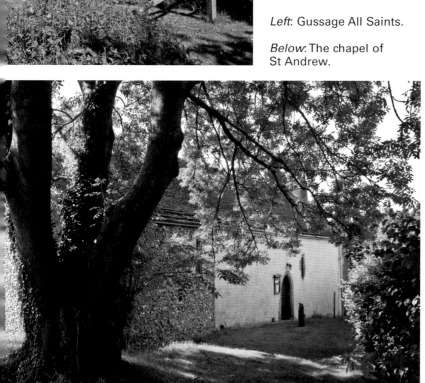

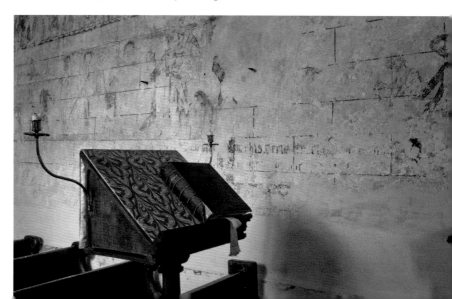

HORTON

A prominent feature within the landscape surrounding the southern edge of the Chase, just a few miles north of Wimborne, is Horton Tower. It was built in the 1700s on a hill overlooking the village by local landowner Humphrey Sturt and is said to have enabled him to watch the hunt across the fields when he became too old to ride. With its seven storeys and a fireplace halfway up, it has been described as the ugliest folly in the county, but as an observatory it must have commanded magnificent views across the Chase, the Stour Valley and maybe even as far as the coast towards the Isle of Wight.

It once featured in the film of Thomas Hardy's *Far from the Madding Crowd*, but this landmark tower has since been fully restored by a telecommunications company and has found a new lease of life in supporting mobile phone communications.

It was in the fields surrounding Horton that a famous capture took place. Just a few days after the fateful Battle of Sedgemoor in 1685 the Duke of Monmouth was found hiding in a ditch under an ash tree dressed as a shepherd. One can only assume he was heading for the coast after his ill-fated attempt to take the throne from James II and return to Holland. To mark the capture the tree became known as 'The Monmouth Ash'. Many years later the original tree died but a sapling was planted to mark the spot and this tree is still growing today.

This tale of the Duke of Monmouth's capture leads us into another fascinating story of a local man from Holt, near Horton, who sent the Duke to trial and his eventual execution just one week after his capture. Anthony Ettricke was a seventeenth-century barrister who served as recorder and magistrate for Wimborne and the surrounding area. Ettricke is perhaps better known as 'The Man in the Wall'. Although a pillar of the community, he was regarded as something of an eccentric and despite all his good work for the church he fell out with the church authorities and swore that when he died he would neither be buried inside Wimborne minster nor its graveyard, and neither above nor below ground.

Eventually, Ettricke made peace with the church but felt as a lawyer he could not go back on his word and arranged for his tomb to be inserted in the wall of the minster, half in and half out and only halfway above ground and halfway below it. A novel solution maybe, but Ettricke had already claimed he would die in 1693 and had the date engraved on his tomb. However, he lived ten years longer than he expected, requiring the date on the tomb to be amended to 1703, something which can clearly be seen on the tomb in Wimborne minster today.

Close to Horton is one of Dorset's largest areas of lowland heathland at Holt Heath. This nature reserve contains examples of common heather, bell heather, cross-leaved heath, sundews and marsh gentian. Birds include large populations of Dartford warbler, stonechat and nightjar and this area is Dorset's only site for breeding curlew.

On the edge of the heath is the community of Woodlands and here is a further tale of the area's links with royalty. On this occasion it is the fifteen-year-old King Edward VI (1537–53), who, it is said, sat under an oak tree during the summer of 1552 and 'touched for King's Evil'. King's Evil was historically the term given to a form of tuberculosis affecting the lymph nodes of the neck. Legend has it that the touch of the King of England or France could cure the disease. How many people were touched by Edward VI is not known but the original tree still retains that secret; it is still standing, supported by cables and is called the 'Remedy Oak'.

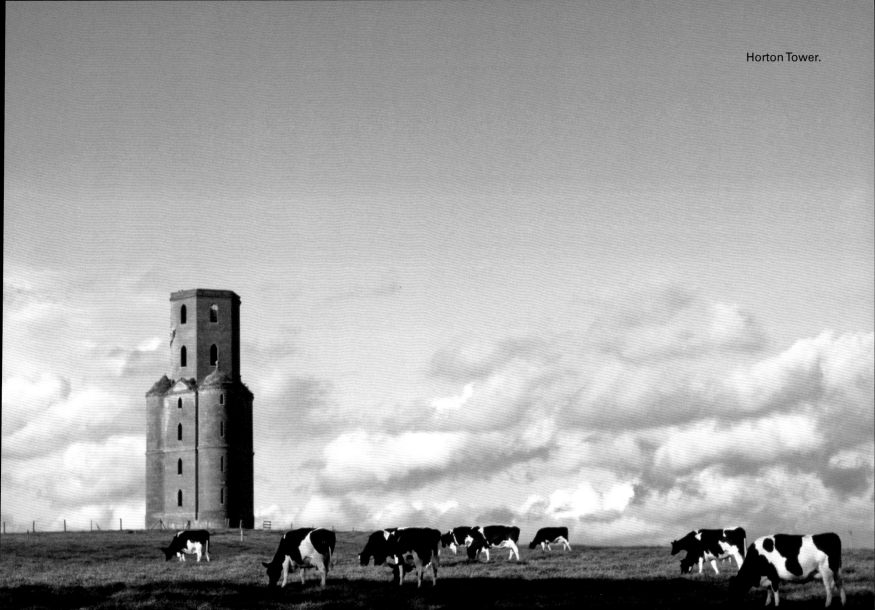

Horton Tower.

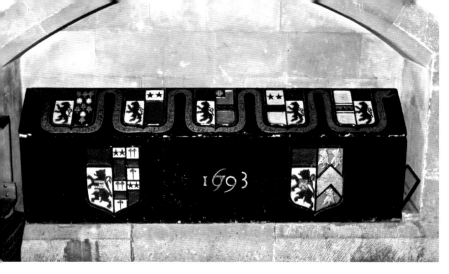

Above: The Ettricke Tomb in Wimborne minster.

Below: The Remedy Oak.

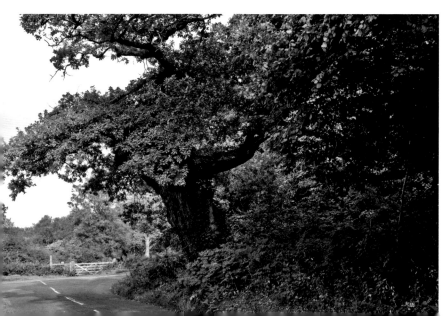

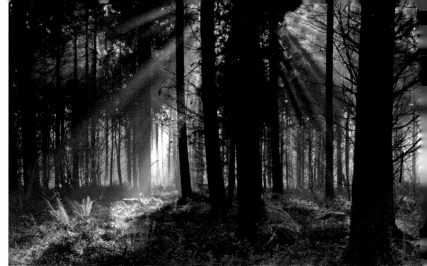

Above: Morning sunbeams in nearby Holt Forest.

Below: Corn stooks near Horton, overlooked by the distant tower. This traditional, more attractive method is employed for thatching purposes.

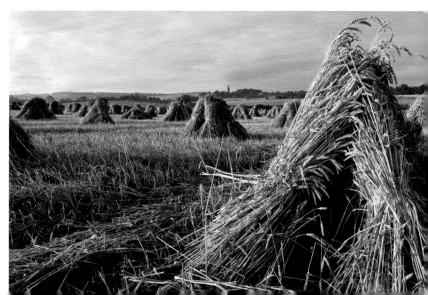

KNOWLTON CHURCH

Standing beside the Wimborne to Cranborne road are the ruins of Knowlton church. Somehow, it feels more suited to the landscape of Cranborne Chase, although geographically its location is just short of the southern inner Chase boundary.

The church was built in the twelfth century, modified in the fourteenth and fifteenth centuries and was used until the seventeenth century by a small riverside hamlet which has since vanished, possibly as a result of the Black Death. It was clearly built within a Neolithic barrow or earth circle, which suggests that in its time it symbolised a transition from Pagan to Christian worship.

Around 1747 the church was given a new roof which very soon collapsed; the building was then left abandoned. Mysterious tales surround this happening and the disappearance of the bell, which local legend suggests was stolen and dumped in White Mill Pool at Sturminster Marshall when the robbers decided they could run no more.

Below left: Knowlton church under a painterly sky.

Below: White Mill near Sturminster Marshall and the mill pond where the bell of Knowlton church is said to have been dumped.

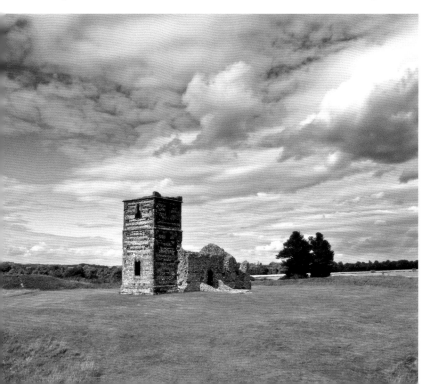

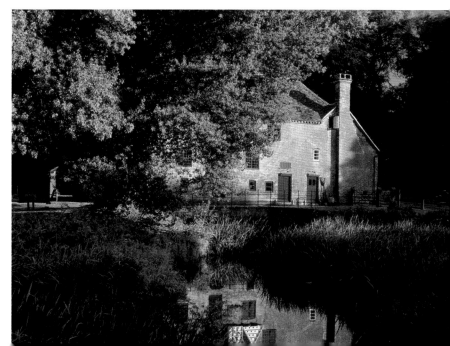

LARMER TREE GARDENS

To describe the existence of pleasure gardens in the midst of the remote and atmospheric landscape of Cranborne Chase may seem rather strange, but they certainly exist and are certainly pleasure gardens.

Just northwest of Farnham are located the Larmer Tree Gardens, described as 'The Jewel of Cranborne Chase'. In 1880, Augustus Lane Fox inherited the Rushmore Estate. As a condition of his inheritance it was necessary for him to change his name to Pitt Rivers and so he became known as Augustus Lane Fox Pitt Rivers. He immediately began creating the Larmer Tree Gardens, named after the tree which formed the ancient boundary between Dorset and Wiltshire. It is thought that the famous tree, possibly a wych elm, was the assembly point for King John and his hunting circle before they set off across the Chase in search of their prey. Pitt Rivers intended the gardens to provide education and enlightenment to visitors and included various structures including an Indian and Nepalese Room acquired after the British Empire exhibition of 1898. A racecourse, tennis courts, golf course and bowling green were also added together with picnic areas complete with chairs, tables and cutlery, all supplied without charge.

Music and entertainment were also provided and on Sunday afternoons in summer a local band would play. In fact I well remember my own grandfather describing his enjoyment of delightful afternoons at the Larmer Tree Gardens when he played in Blandford Forum's own town band.

A singing theatre and plays were also performed in the open air and in the evenings the gardens were illuminated by thousands of hanging lamps lit by candles for open-air dancing. In 1895, Thomas Hardy visited the gardens and danced with Pitt Rivers' daughter, Agnes, describing the gardens as 'Quite the prettiest sight I ever saw in my life'.

By 1899, the gardens were attracting 40,000 people a year. With Pitt Rivers' death in 1900 the gardens closed, and both they and the buildings fell into decay.

In 1991, under the direction of Augustus Pitt Rivers' great-grandson Michael Pitt Rivers, a restoration programme was started, resulting in the gardens reopening to the public in 1995. A new Larmer Tree was also planted to mark the new millennium in 1999.

Today the gardens still contain the Nepalese Room, Roman temple and Colonial style pavilion. The open-air theatre has a backdrop painted by the scenery department of the Welsh National Opera and the lawns and gardens with their striding peacocks provide a colourful backdrop to the annual Larmer Tree Music Festival.

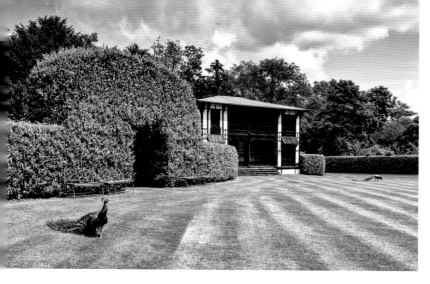

Above: Peacocks parade in the Larmer Tree Gardens in front of the Lower Indian Room.

Below: The temple viewed from the steps to the dell.

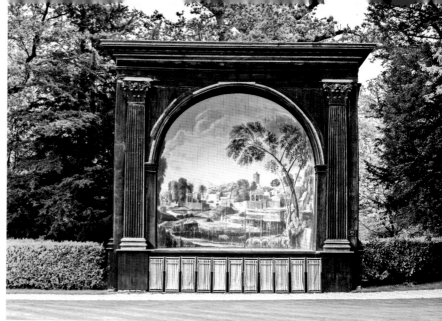

Above: The Singing Theatre.

Right: The temple viewed from the dell.

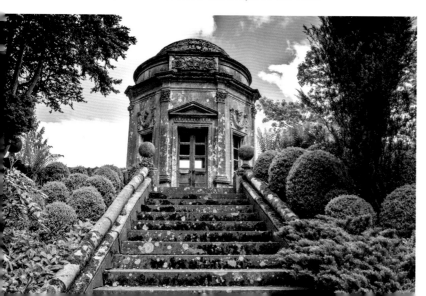

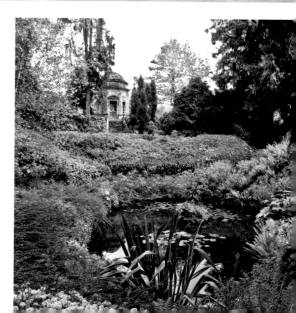

MARTIN

On the eastern boundary lies the village of Martin, which is actually in the neighbouring county of Hampshire. However, the landscape of Martin Down is very much a part of the Chase.

As a National Nature Reserve it is one of the largest areas of chalk downland in the country and includes grassland habitats, scrub and woodland which provide a wide range of downland flowers, insects, birds and wildlife. Common grazing rights still exist on Martin Down as indeed they have since medieval times.

The village contains many picturesque cottages, some dating back to the fifteenth century, set out along the main street. The village green is also a welcome feature, together with the spired church with parts dating back to the Norman era.

Within the churchyard is a memorial to shepherd William Lawes, who died in 1886 at the age of eighty-six. He provided a lifetime of memories for W.H. Hudson's classic *A Shepherd's Life*. William Lawes became 'Isaac Bawcombe' and the village of Martin the 'Winterbourne Bishop' of the book.

A colourful corner in the village of Martin.

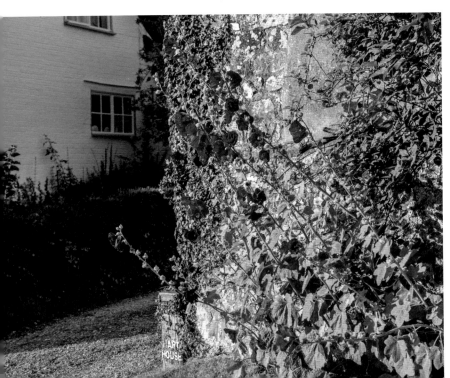

Martin's spired Norman church of All Saints.

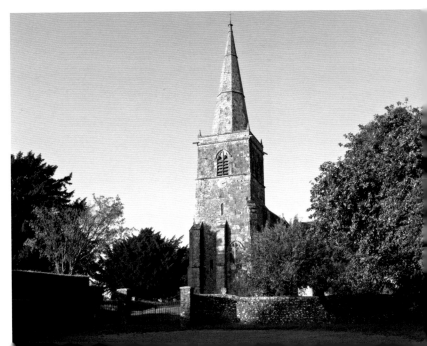

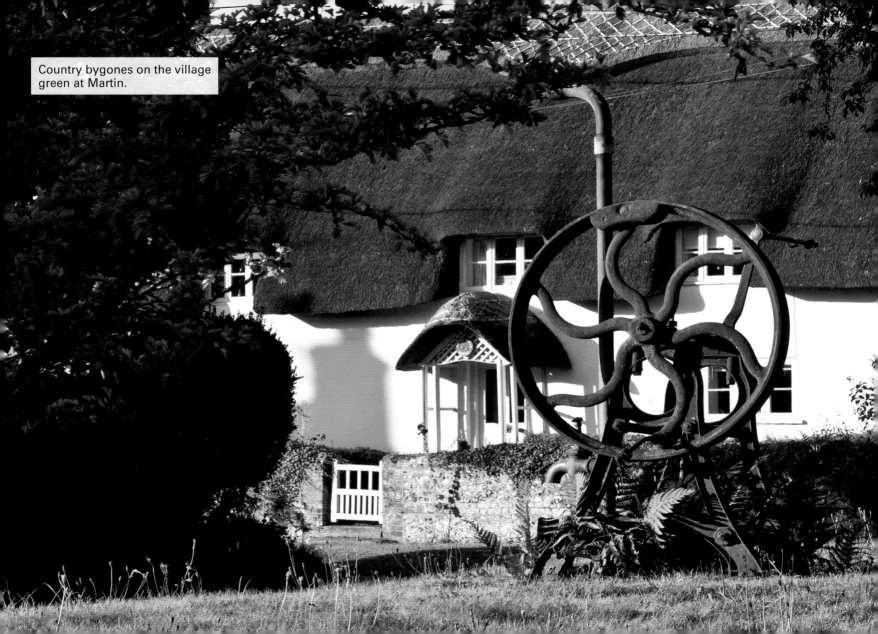

Country bygones on the village green at Martin.

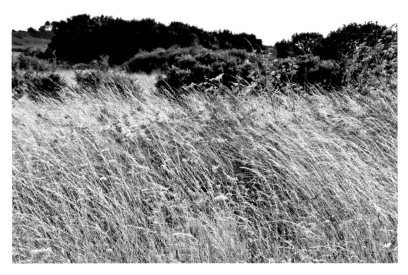

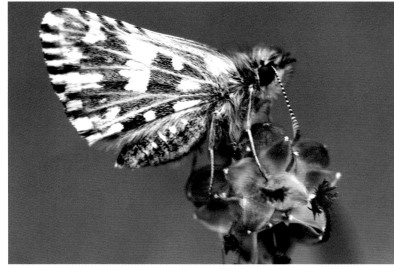

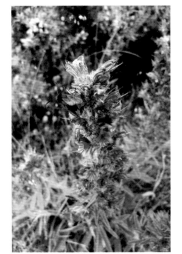

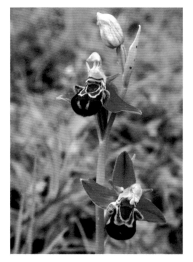

Above: High summer on Martin Down. (*Courtesy of Tony Bates*)

Left: Viper's bugloss (*Echium vulgari*) and Six-Spot burnet moth (*Zygaena Filipendulae*). (*Courtesy of Tony Bates*)

Above: Grizzled Skipper butterfly (*Pyrgus malvae*). (*Courtesy of Tony Bates*)

Left: Bee orchid (*Ophrys apifera*). (*Courtesy of Tony Bates*)

MELBURY ABBAS

Settled under the great chalk hills which rise to over 860 feet at Melbury Beacon, the village has many ancient cottages and is reached from nearby Shaftesbury through a deep tree-covered cutting. The road out is via the infamous and steep Spreadeagle Hill. From the top of Spreadeagle is one of Dorset's most magnificent views. To the east lies the start of Cranborne Chase, Win Green and the Wiltshire border and to the west can be seen the Stour Valley and the distant Dorset vales.

It was in Melbury Abbas on 11 February 1800 that William Henry Fox Talbot was born into a well-to-do family who had owned Lacock abbey in Wiltshire since the 1500s. William of course later became an MP, scientist, innovator and pioneer of photography.

Unfortunately, Melbury Abbas did not keep the young Fox Talbot for long; his father died heavily in debt before William was one year old, forcing him and his mother to live in a variety of homes until she remarried in 1804. It appears Fox Talbot's mother was a remarkable woman, eventually managing the Lacock estate to such effect they were able to return there. Lacock later became famous as the home where Fox Talbot would carry out his first photographic experiments.

From East Melbury a road reaches the summit of the Downs, up what is known as Zig Zag Hill. This is a sound piece of alpine road construction, taking the traveller through the gradients in a series of five hairpin bends. This road travels through fine beech woods, providing a canopy of green in summer and glorious colour in autumn.

Melbury Hill rises above the village, seen here in the winter.

Looking down on Melbury Abbas from Melbury Hill in early autumn. The beech woods above the village contain the famous Zig Zag Hill.

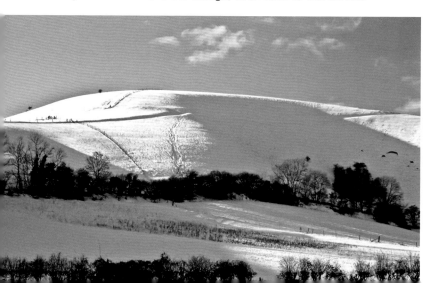

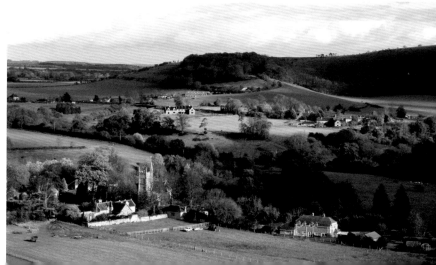

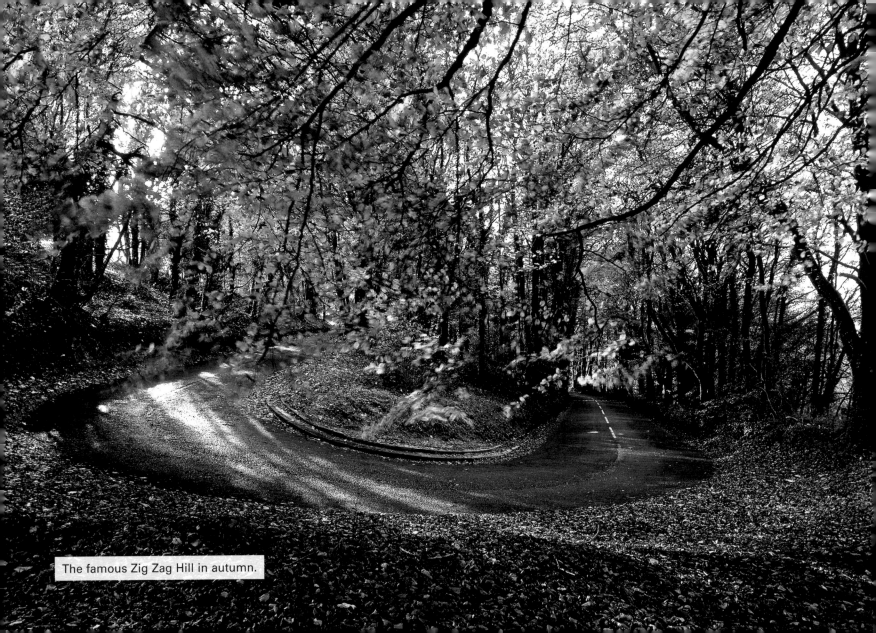

The famous Zig Zag Hill in autumn.

NADDER VALLEY

For the purposes of this book the River Nadder forms the northern rim of my Cranborne Chase outer boundary and is itself an attractive and historical area of exploration. The quarries at Chilmark, for example, provided the stone for the building of Salisbury Cathedral just 12 miles away. These locations trace Wiltshire's Nadder Valley just north of Shaftesbury on the northwest fringe through to Salisbury in the east.

Below right: The majestic gateway to the Fonthill Estate.

Below: The magnificent spire of Salisbury Cathedral marks the northeastern boundary of the Chase and where the River Nadder meets the River Avon.

The Fonthill Estate

We start this area of exploration with the Fonthill Estate which lies on the northern side of the Nadder Valley between Tisbury and the unspoilt villages of Hindon, Fonthill Bishop and Fonthill Gifford. The Fonthill Estate contains a beautiful tree-fringed lake with an entrance through a majestic gateway believed to be the work of renowned architect Inigo Jones.

The attractive lake is over a mile in length and was used for the river scenes in the award-winning film *Chocolat* starring Juliette Binoche, Johnny Depp and Judi Dench. The film was based on the romantic novel by Joanne Harris.

Over the years the Fonthill estate has a fascinating architectural history, with many grand country houses being built on the estate, not least of which was Fonthill abbey.

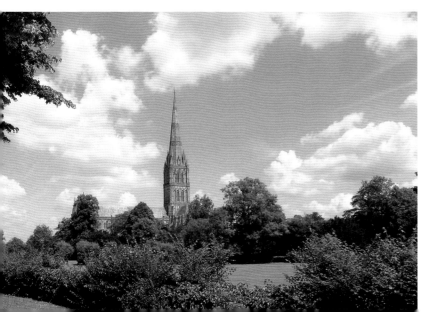

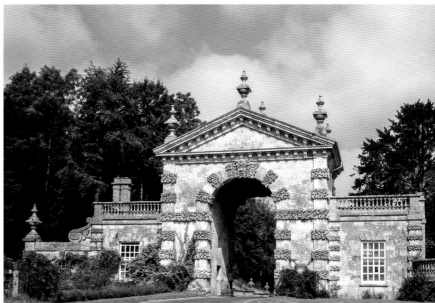

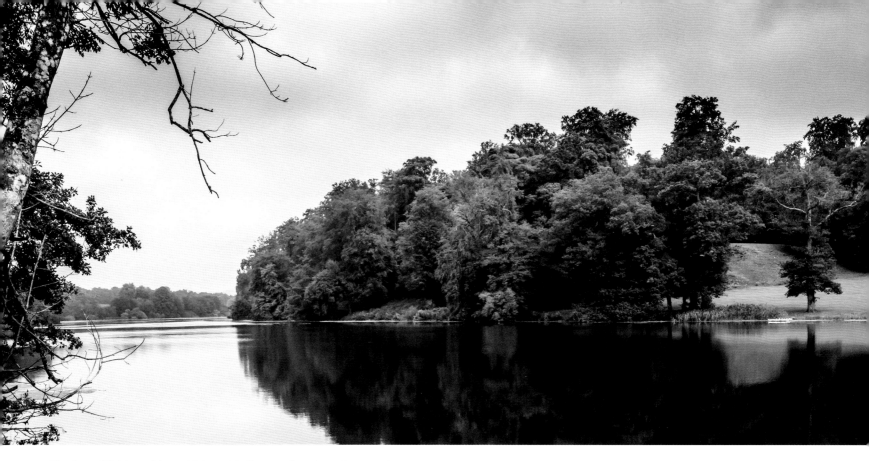

The beautiful tree-fringed lake with tinges of early autumn colour.

This was a Gothic style property designed like a cathedral and commissioned by a rich and somewhat eccentric author, William Beckford Jnr. Beckford had inherited the estate and a not insignificant fortune from his father, William Beckford, a former Lord Mayor of London. The design of the abbey was in such grandiose form that the tower or spire was intended to be 450 feet high, dwarfing Salisbury Cathedral's spire by around 50 feet. Never completed, the spire collapsed through faulty workmanship which damaged most of the building, the remains of which are hidden from view today.

Old Wardour Castle

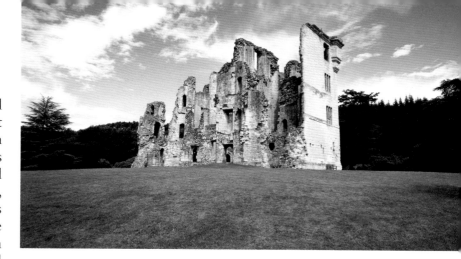

Set on the northern perimeter of the outer Chase within beautiful Wiltshire countryside just 15 miles west of Salisbury is what is now known as Old Wardour Castle. Built in the fourteenth century by Lord Lovell with permission from Richard II, it is said to have been modelled on a French design and described as a dwelling rather than a castle built for defence. In 1461, the Lovells lost the castle and it passed through several owners until being bought by Sir Thomas Arundell in 1544. The castle home of the Arundells came under threat in April 1643 from around 1,300 Parliamentarians, led by Sir Edward Hungerford and Gen. Edmund Ludlow, who attempted to seize the property due to the Arundells' close associations with the King.

Lord Arundell was away at the time leaving only his wife, household staff and twenty-five troops who heroically withstood the attack for several days. Finally, Hungerford ordered his troops to lay mines beneath the castle walls but incredibly the castle withstood the effect. After weeks of resistance, Lady Arundell was eventually forced to surrender to the Parliamentary forces in May 1643.

In December 1643 Henry, the new Lord Arundell and heir to the estate, led a Royalist assault on Wardour in an attempt to regain the family home. The battle raged for several months until Arundell, in one last desperate attempt to free the family home of Parliamentarians, ordered gunpowder to be placed at strategic points with devastating effect.

Today the site is under the control of English Heritage and even in ruins it remains an imposing sight, standing alone in an expanse of lush green landscape, the white stone contrasting well with its surroundings.

Above: The imposing ruins of Old Wardour Castle.

Right: The ruined interior of Old Wardour Castle.

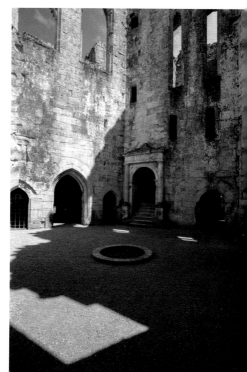

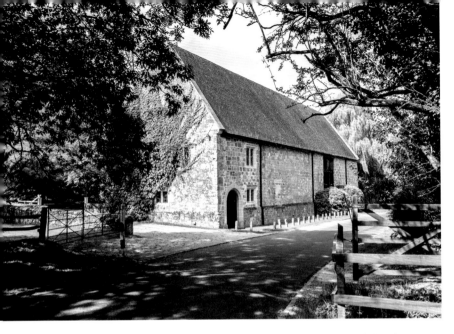

During the 1990s the castle became an important setting for the film *Robin Hood: Prince of Thieves*, starring Kevin Costner.

Ansty

Ansty lies towards the northern boundary of the Chase, though it has never been under the jurisdiction of the Chase laws. There has been a settlement here for over 1,000 years and today, situated among the downland and woods with its manor house, spring fed pond and attractive church of St James, which dates from 1230, it remains very characteristic of a Chase village.

Cottages and thatched roofs abound throughout the narrow lanes. The manor house was once owned by the Turberville family, who gave it to the Order of the Knights Hospitallers in 1211. The order was part of Ansty for 300 years, caring for the local quarrymen and masons employed in the building of Salisbury Cathedral in addition to pilgrims, hunters and workers of Cranborne Chase.

There is a brief mention of Ansty in Thomas Hardy's *Tess of the d'Urbervilles*, no doubt inspired by the name of the former Turberville family.

Perhaps the most striking aspect is the ancient pond, complete with an historic maypole standing alongside at the junction of the main street and a lane leading to Ansty Coombe. The Ansty maypole is famous throughout the county; it has been in existence since the sixteenth century.

Earlier maypoles have been much higher than the current example; in fact, Ansty once claimed to have the highest maypole in the country at almost 100 feet, but the last pole was blown down in a gale in 1993, its replacement being a much safer 50 feet

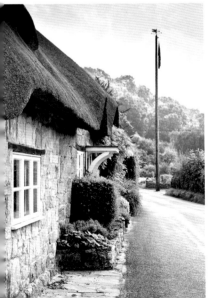

Above: This renovated building is believed to stand on the site of the Knights Hospitaller's Hospice and was built in 1596 by Thomas Arundell, probably as a banqueting hall.

Left: Ansty's famous maypole, located in the centre of a road junction in the high street.

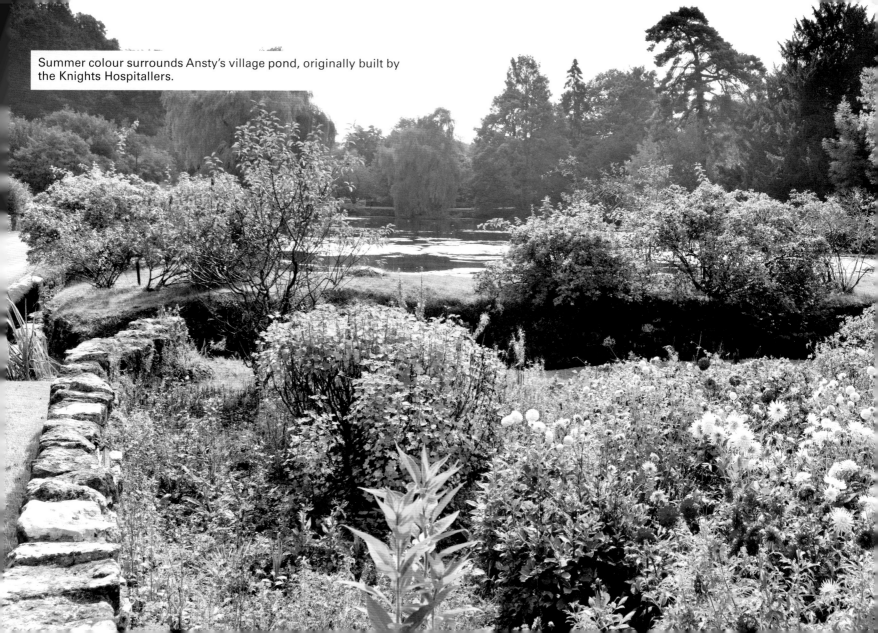

Summer colour surrounds Ansty's village pond, originally built by the Knights Hospitallers.

high but still allowing the continuation of the annual May Day celebrations. Traditionally, the maypole is replaced every twenty years and must be in place between sunrise and sunset in one day in order to preserve the right to have it positioned in the road in the centre of the village.

Even the local hostelry, the Arundell Inn, was renamed 'The Maypole Inn' but unfortunately no longer features in the May Day celebrations as it is now a private house.

Semley

This village takes its name from the River Sem, which meets the River Nadder just outside the village. This area was once an important dairy farming community with its own dairy and railway station, which distributed local milk and produce direct to the London markets. After more than 100 years of operation the station closed in 1966 and the former buildings and dairy depot have since found new life as period antiques.

One of the most attractive features of Semley is the Common. Over 300 acres in size, Semley Common stretches for almost a mile from outside the church of St Leonard. The land was a gift from Queen Elizabeth I in 1572 to the Arundell family, whose descendants still retain the freehold. Commoners grazed their cattle, pigs and sheep here, but today it is an area of recreation and wildlife conservation.

The church of St Leonard provides two poignant memorials to Semley inhabitants. In the churchyard is an impressive bronze

Church Farm and common seen from the churchyard.

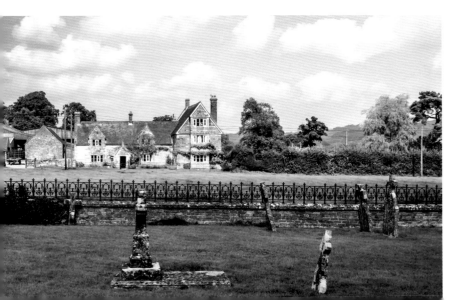

The elegant bronze memorial to Lt George Dewrance against the backdrop of the Wiltshire landscape.

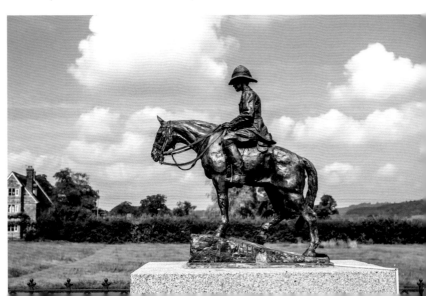

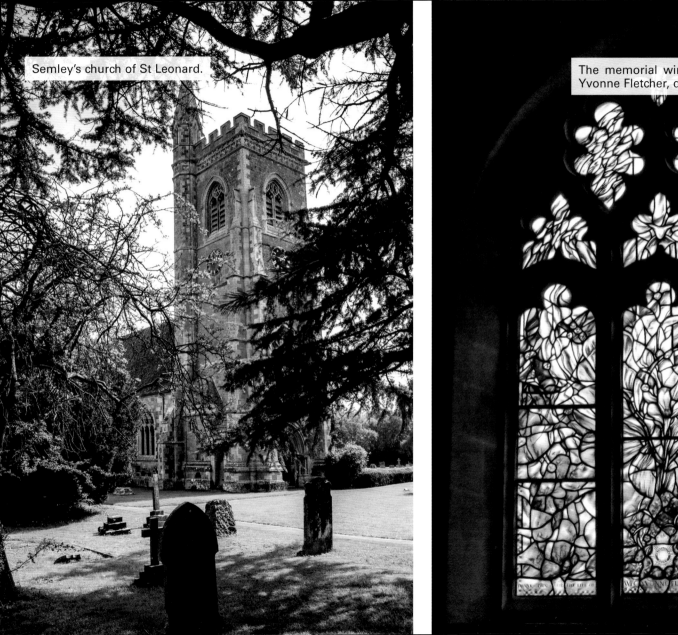

Semley's church of St Leonard.

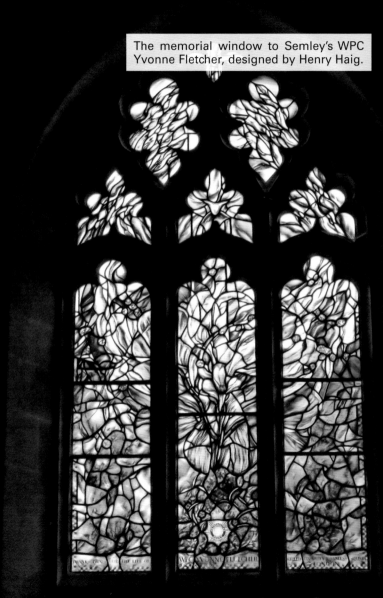

The memorial window to Semley's WPC Yvonne Fletcher, designed by Henry Haig.

soldier on horseback as a memorial to Lt George Dewrance, who died at the age of thirty-six in the First World War. In the Lady chapel is a beautiful stained-glass window designed by Henry Haig in memory of WPC Yvonne Fletcher, who was shot and killed in the Libyan Embassy siege in London in 1984.

Semley has also been the home of English actor Robert Morley (1908–92), who was born in the village, and famous classical guitarist Julian Bream, who lived in a Georgian farmhouse for over forty years before moving to nearby Donhead St Andrew.

Fovant

The village of Fovant lies on the northern fringe of Cranborne Chase, directly on the A30 between Salisbury and Shaftesbury. It is perhaps most famous for the military badges carved into the chalk hillside above the village. I remember being frequently taken to view these badges as a small boy by my grandfather, who had a fascination with them. To him it was almost a pilgrimage to remember some of his young Dorset friends who never came back from the First World War.

It was during the First World War that both Fovant and nearby Compton Chamberlayne were surrounded by a huge military training camp and here thousands of soldiers from many regiments, including British and Australian units, received their training before being sent off to the battlefields. Many of course did not return and it was to their memory these badges were carved in chalk by their comrades. By the end of the war there were twenty regimental badges carved into the hillside. The church of St George in the village of Fovant also has rows of war graves of British and Australian soldiers.

The famous regimental badges designed in chalk above Fovant. (*Courtesy of Kay Browning*)

The River Nadder flows through a lush wooded landscape between Fovant and Compton Chamberlayne.

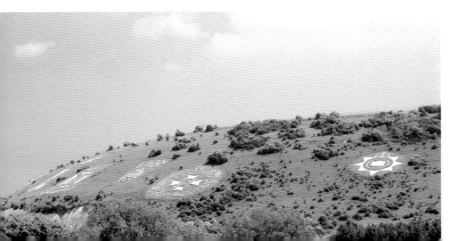

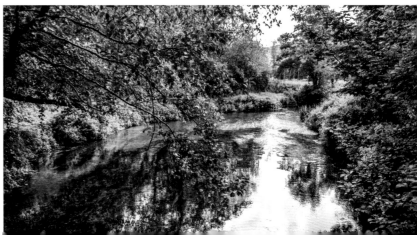

During the Second World War the badges were allowed to become overgrown to prevent them being used as landmarks by the Luftwaffe. Unfortunately, some did not survive this period, but after the war members of the local Home Guard formed an Old Comrades Association, taking on the considerable task of restoring the badges and adding two new emblems of Wiltshire regiments. Today there is no sign of the huge military installation of those times, but eight badges have survived and continue to be maintained by members of the Fovant Badges Society.

Wilton House

Wilton House has been home to the Earls of Pembroke since the 1540s and today is the home of the 18th Earl of Pembroke. The house and estate are surrounded by beautiful Wiltshire countryside through which flows the River Nadder.

The Palladian Bridge crosses the River Nadder.

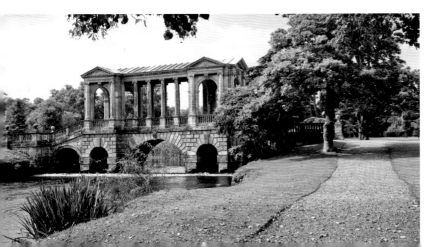

Set in 21 acres of parkland and gardens, it was built on the site of a ninth-century nunnery founded by King Alfred, later replaced by a twelfth-century Benedictine abbey which was surrendered to Henry V111 in 1539 during the Dissolution of the Monasteries.

Sir William Herbert was the 1st Earl of Pembroke, who in 1534 married the sister of Catharine Parr, Henry VIII's last wife. He built the original Wilton House in the 1540s after receiving Wilton and much of the estate from the King. However, the house was almost completely destroyed by fire in 1647. A new house was built soon after by Inigo Jones and following his death in 1652 John Webb completed the work. Since then, many earls of Pembroke have added to the original design and between 1987 and 1992, the 17th Earl commissioned a major restoration of both the inside and outside of the building.

The park itself contains some superb cedars with magnificent lawns sweeping down to the River Nadder, across which stands an elegant Palladian bridge built in 1737.

The house contains a seventeenth-century interior and a world-famous art collection with paintings by Van Dyck, Peter Brueghel, Rembrandt and Richard Wilson.

It is not surprising that such a setting has attracted film crews from around the world and such films as *Sense and Sensibility*, *Pride and Prejudice*, *The Madness of King George*, *Mrs Brown* and *The Young Victoria* have all been filmed here.

The house also played an important role in wartime Britain when it was requisitioned as the headquarters of Southern Command in 1940. Much of the planning for D-Day was carried out at Wilton and more than 750 miles of telephone cable were laid in and around the estate, linking the headquarters with vital points in the area.

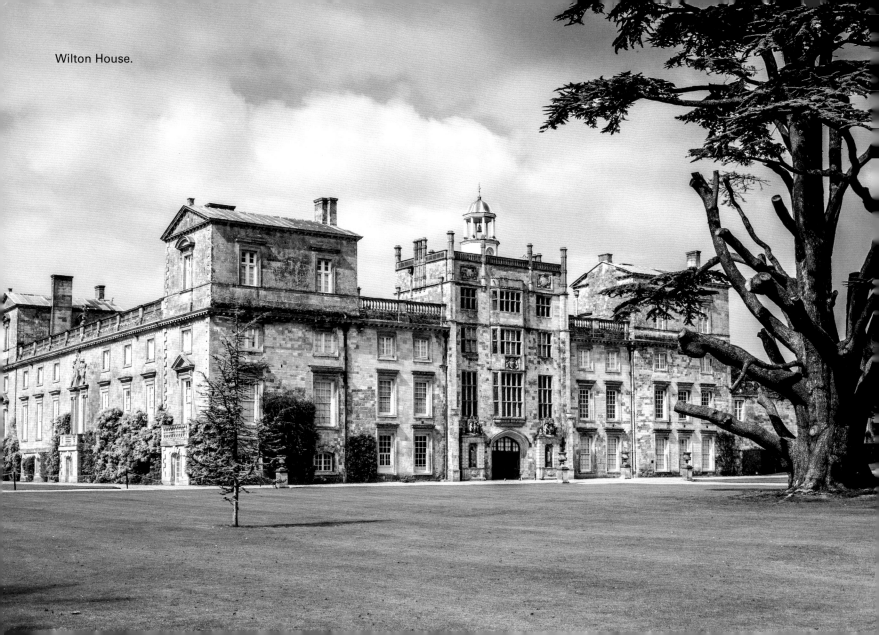

Wilton House.

OX DROVE

The Ox Drove's origin is considered to be a prehistoric ridgeway and would have been one of the main east–west travelling routes for trade during the Bronze Age. It later became a means of moving livestock and following the advent of the turnpike road system and later the railways reverted to its original use by local farmers. Today it forms a most suitable walking trail with distant views of the Cranborne Chase landscape.

The roughly 9-mile stretch from Win Green to Broadchalke is superb in this respect, with distant chalk downland views into Wiltshire linking the Chalke valley views to those of the north. On a clear day the sweeping landscape of the Chase is always present. To the southeast are the distant views of the Solent and the Isle of Wight, with the rest of the rural Dorset landscape stretching as far as Portland in the southwest.

The rural ambience along the Ox Drove leaves the mind to wander back in time to a landscape which has seemingly changed little since hawkers, pedlars and even smugglers would have passed along the route with all manner of provisions, both legal and otherwise. The drove is also intersected by the Roman Ackling Dyke near to Ebblake and again near Win Green, allowing the mind to visualise legions of Roman soldiers passing through.

It is a wonderful place to experience silence as, for much of the way, the Ox Drove passes through hedgerows which in summer are bright with wild flowers. Even within the occasional woodlands, which provide a brief canopy of green, the silence can only be broken by the song of birds enjoying life along this natural sanctuary.

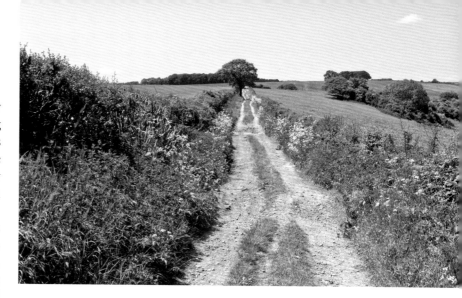

Above: The Ox Drove above Bowerchalke.

Below: Views of Cranborne Chase from the Ox Drove.

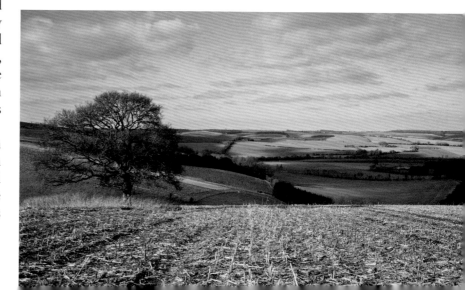

PENTRIDGE

Under the deep escarpment of Pentridge Hill is one of the few 'dead end' villages in Dorset. Here a lane from the A354 Blandford to Salisbury road stops under the hill beside the church, surrounded by Bronze Age barrows and Celtic fields. Close by is Bokerley Dyke, a 5 mile defensive ditch thought to have been dug by the Romano-British in an attempt to keep out Saxon invaders. However, more recent suggestions state this to be more likely of Bronze Age origin.

The village name however derives from the Celtic *pen* meaning hill and *twrch* meaning boar, hence 'hill of the wild boar', although it was first recorded as 'Pentric'.

The church itself was rebuilt in the nineteenth century using some of the original material, largely flint and brick, and is dedicated to St Rumbold.

Of particular interest to me as someone with a lifelong involvement in aviation is the grave by the porch and the window dedicated to Bee Beamont, noted for being the first Briton to fly faster than sound. He retired to Cross Cottage at Pentridge after flying Hurricanes in the Battle of Britain before going on to become one of Britain's most distinguished military test pilots. Tempest, Typhoon, Hunter, Canberra and Britain's first supersonic jet fighter, the English Electric P1 Lightning, were all taken into the skies by 'Roly' Beamont, whose daring antics with the rather cumbersome Canberra bomber at Farnborough

Summer sky over the heights of Pentridge.

Pentridge, the parish church of St Rumbold.

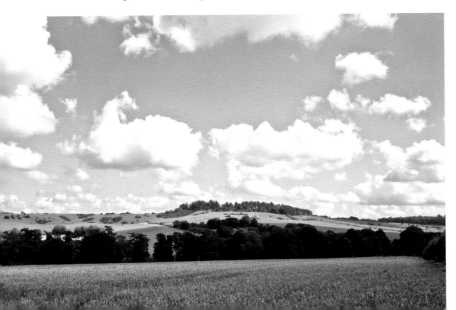

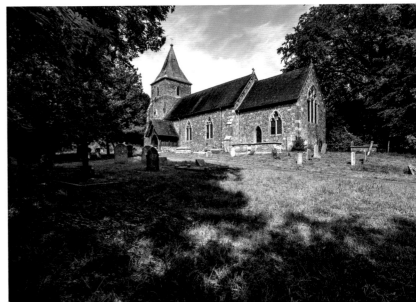

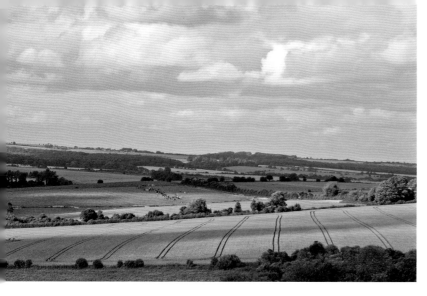

Above: Looking north from Pentridge.

Below: Pimperne Long Barrow.

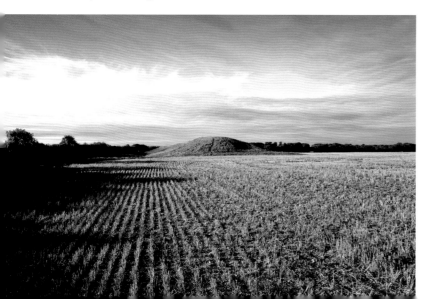

air shows became legendary along with his 'sit on the tail' fast climbs with the P1 Lightning.

Another item is a memorial to a certain Mr Browning of Woodyates, who died in 1746. His son was the innkeeper of the Woodyates Inn, once located back on the main road but now no longer. The innkeeper's great-grandson was another Robert Browning, whose fame as a poet still lives on.

The views from Pentridge Hill are some of the most memorable on the Chase with a panorama of wide open vistas and huge skies in all directions.

PIMPERNE

The village of Pimperne sits on the road north of Blandford Forum before it reaches out on to the Chase landscape.

The village is surrounded by Iron and Bronze Age settlements with one thought to date from 500 BC. On the northern boundary is Pimperne's Long Barrow. It is considered to be the largest in the country at 354 feet long and 92 feet wide and is around 4,000 years old.

There was originally an Anglo-Saxon church on the site but this was taken down and rebuilt in 1873 by local benefactor Lord Portman, who incorporated parts of the original Norman church. Charles Kingsley, author of *The Water-Babies*, was Rector here during the 1840s.

ROCKBOURNE ROMAN VILLA

Rockbourne is an attractive village on the eastern fringe of Cranborne Chase and lies within the Hampshire boundary.

Just south of the village is a remarkable find in a peaceful rural setting. Rockbourne Roman villa is a courtyard villa discovered in 1942 and now on public display. This exceptional find is due to a local farmer's adventurous ferret that became trapped in a rabbit warren. During the rescue operation, the farmer, Mr Morley Hewitt, discovered traces of oyster shells and tiles. Realising the importance of this discovery, Morley Hewitt attempted a further excavation only to find a mosaic floor. As this happened during the war years, a full scale excavation did not take place until 1956, with further work continuing through to 1982.

This has resulted in Rockbourne's Roman villa being assessed as the largest known villa in the area and with a history dating from the Iron Age to the fifth century AD. It is now possible to view the extent of the villa with its forty rooms, bathhouses, workshops, underfloor heating system and magnificent mosaics. Many artefacts including skeletons and jewellery can be seen in the on-site museum together with a history of the excavations.

Pimperne, the village church of St Peter.

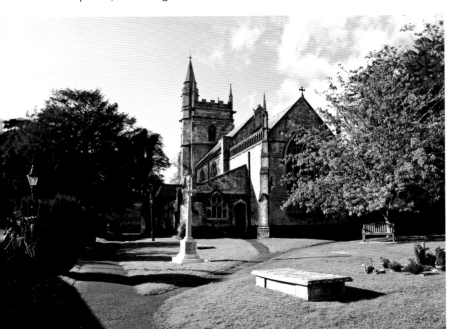

An unusual sight in the fields north of Pimperne, a Ferris wheel appears above the fields in the direction of Tarrant Hinton in readiness for the annual Great Dorset Steam Fair.

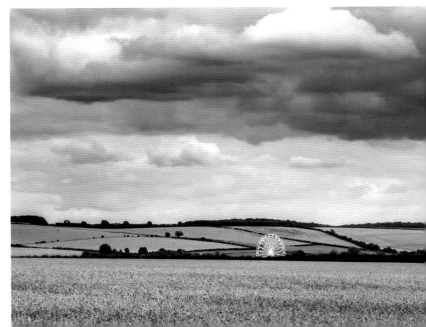

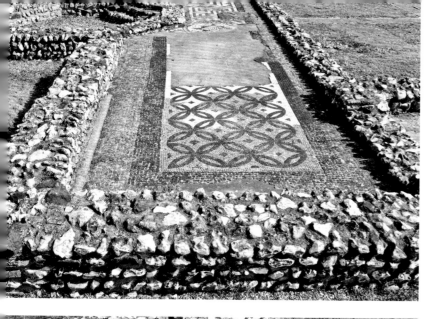

Above left: It was here that the first discoveries were made by Mr Morley Hewitt in 1942 when his initial excavation revealed the mosaic design of the Roman bathing area (the east bath suite).

Below left: The hypocaust or underfloor heating system built from curved roof tiles.

Below: Roman mosaic in the *triclinium* or dining room.

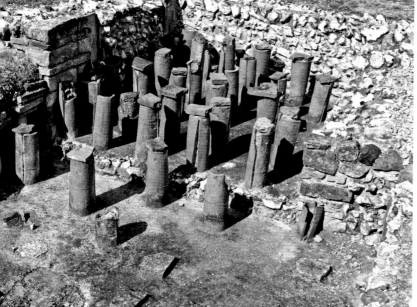

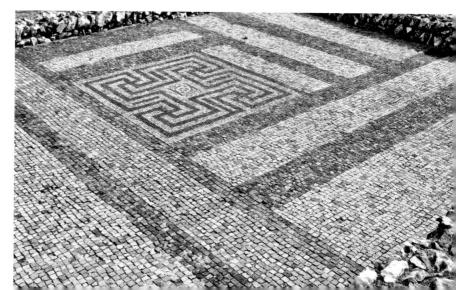

SHAFTESBURY

Shaftesbury is located on the outer boundary of the Chase and situated at more than 750 feet is the only ancient hilltop town in Dorset. Commanding views across the Blackmore Vale and into the neighbouring counties of Wiltshire and Somerset, it was once described by venerable writer of English history Arthur Mee as one of the finest natural thrones in Dorset. It also became 'Shaston' in Thomas Hardy's novels. He described it as 'one of the queerest and quaintest spots with a limitless landscape'. It remains one of the oldest and highest towns in England.

The steep and cobbled Gold Hill is known across the world for having been featured in several historic film dramas. It was also the chosen location for the famous Ridley Scott directed television commercial for Hovis Bread which was made in 1973.

Actor Robert Newton, famous for his portrayal of Long John Silver in *Treasure Island* and as Fagan in David Lean's 1948 film *Oliver Twist* was born in the town.

It was the Saxons who first founded a hilltop town here because of its strategic position overlooking a wide landscape. King Alfred also made Shaftesbury a defensive town after his defeat of the Vikings and due to its secure position he founded an abbey here for his daughter.

The foundation of the abbey led to prosperity for the town and three royal mints were established, which struck silver coins bearing the town's name.

The original abbey was founded in AD 888 and became the wealthiest Benedictine nunnery in England, but was destroyed in 1539 by Thomas Cromwell under orders from Henry VIII.

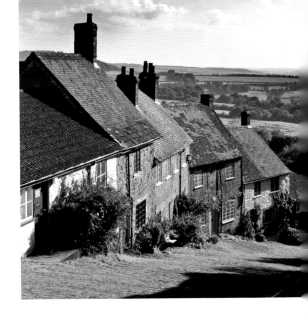

Shaftesbury's famous Gold Hill with the landscape beyond.

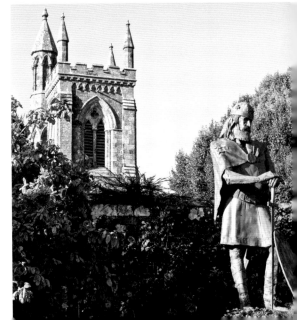

King Alfred in the Abbey Museum Gardens with the tower of Holy Trinity church in the background.

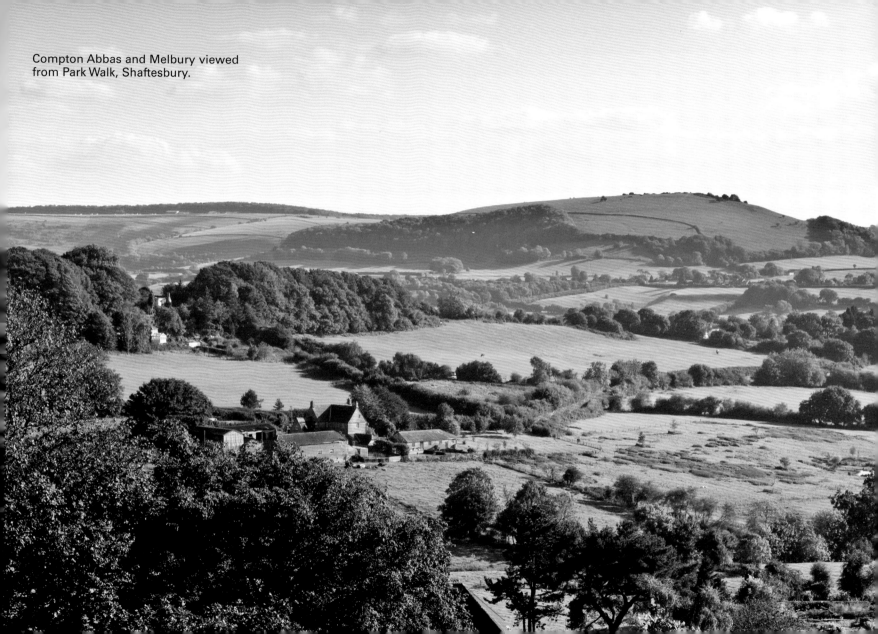

Compton Abbas and Melbury viewed
from Park Walk, Shaftesbury.

The Abbey Museum and Gardens provide an ideal place to view the ruins and from Park Walk the surrounding landscape is superb.

In 981 the corpse of Edward the Martyr was taken to Shaftesbury abbey from Wareham after his murder at Corfe Castle. Following this burial, the town became known as Edwardstowe for a while, but soon reverted to Shaftesbury once the pilgrimages to the martyr's tomb became less of a feature.

King Canute also found Shaftesbury to be a suitable inland resting place far from the coast; he died here in 1035 but is buried in Winchester.

SIXPENNY HANDLEY

This village sits on the Chase between the Romano-British village of Woodcutts and the Roman Road of Ackling Dyke and provides the only shops for miles around.

The name has been the subject of much interpretation but the somewhat whimsical version of '6d Handley', which once appeared on signposts has no monetary significance whatsoever. The name is derived from two Saxon land divisions – 'hundreds' – called 'Sexpenna' and 'Hanlega', meaning 'united'.

Consumed by several fires, the village experienced the last of these in 1892, leaving more than 200 people homeless, prior to which most of the buildings were destroyed. The church survived however, and registers here record the marriage of Isaac Gulliver, Dorset's most famous smuggler, in 1768.

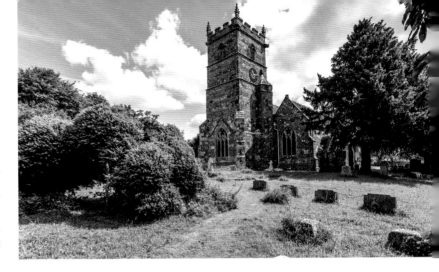

Above: St Mary's church and churchyard, which has had considerable success in the 'Living Churchyard Competition', organised jointly by the Salisbury Diocese and the Dorset Wildlife Trust.

Below: One of the many trails through Garston Wood, seen here in the dappled light of early spring.

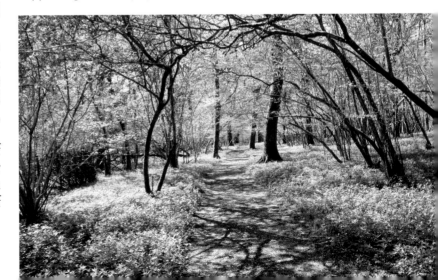

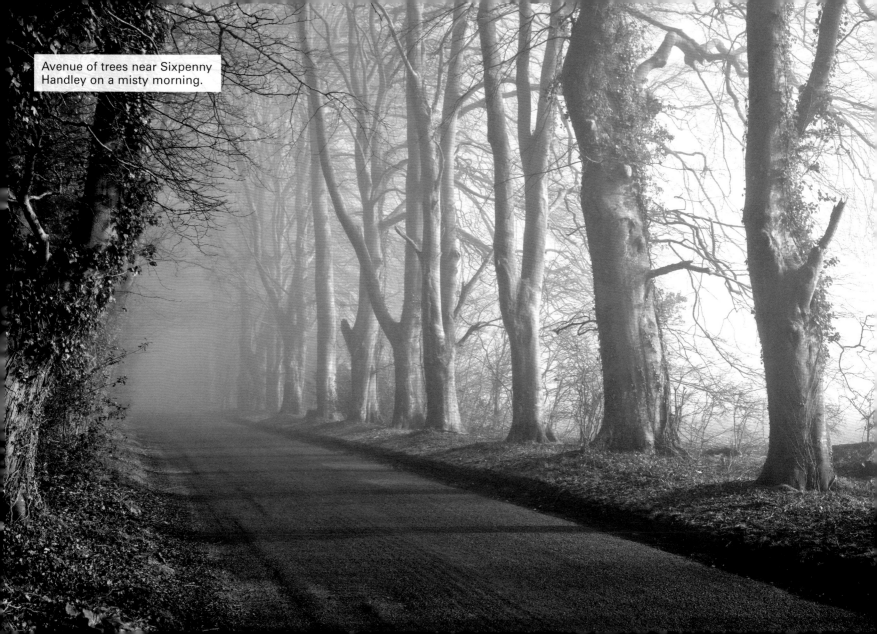

Avenue of trees near Sixpenny Handley on a misty morning.

A further reminder of the lawless activities of the Chase was found on a tombstone in the churchyard stating,

This stone was the cover of the tomb which was removed to afford space for the enlargement of the church in 1879 when deer stealing was prevalent. The deer stealers used to remove it to place in the tomb the deer they had taken till they had the opportunity to remove them.

Near Sixpenny Handley is the RSPB Nature Reserve of Garston Wood. This site has been managed by the RSPB since 1986. With paths and rides crisscrossing the wood, there is much to experience throughout the seasons.

In spring and summer, the wood is carpeted with a magnificent display of wild flowers: bluebells, ransomes, wood anemone and early purple orchids. Butterflies are also prevalent here and twenty-seven species have been recorded, together with seventy-one species of bird which bring the woodland to life with their song. However, there are also times when all you can hear is silence and the rustling of leaves in the canopy above. The majority of Garston Wood is ancient woodland, which has played an important role in providing hazel for hurdle fencing and thatching spars for hundreds of years and continues to do so today.

THE TARRANT VALLEY

Within the boundaries of Cranborne Chase a small chalk stream rises below the heights of Ashmore at Stubhampton Bottom and flows south through a peaceful valley harbouring a series of villages. Its name is the Tarrant and the valley is the Tarrant Valley. The villages are Tarrant Gunville, Tarrant Hinton, Tarrant Launceston, Tarrant Monkton, Tarrant Rawston, Tarrant Rushton, Tarrant Keyneston and Tarrant Crawford. It is at Tarrant Crawford that the Tarrant meets the Dorset Stour, following a journey through rural pastures and landscapes where village after village has adopted its name.

The Tarrant at Tarrant Crawford.

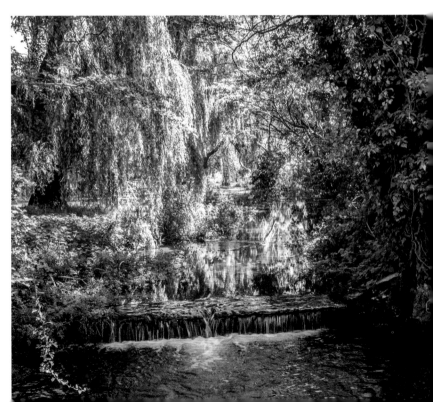

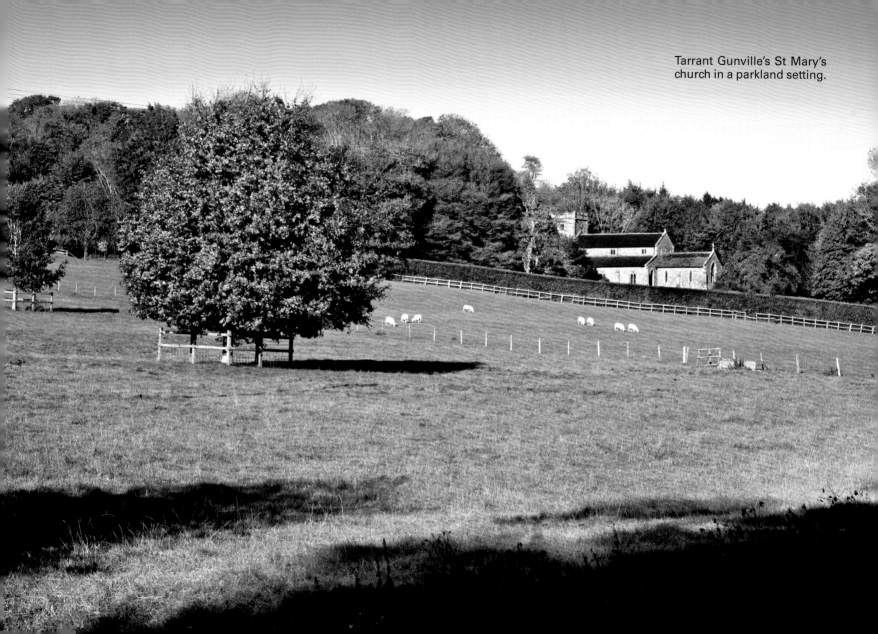

Tarrant Gunville's St Mary's church in a parkland setting.

Tarrant Gunville

Tarrant Gunville spreads itself along a single lane with many attractive thatched cottages and glimpses of its church of St Mary, which was rebuilt in the nineteenth century.

The village was the home of Josiah Wedgewood II, son of Josiah Wedgewood the famous potter. His brother Thomas also lived in the village for five years prior to his death at the young age of thirty-four and is buried in St Mary's churchyard. Thomas was one of photography's pioneers when he became the first to use silver nitrate on paper exposed to sunlight in order to provide an image. Unfortunately, he was unable to fix the image, leaving this element of the process to Fox Talbot and others to perfect.

In parkland to the east of the village are the remains of Eastbury House, once one of Dorset's finest Georgian stately homes. It was built for George Doddington, Lord of the Admiralty in 1718, by Sir John Vanbrugh, who designed Blenheim and Castle Howard. It was completed in 1738 but had something of a chequered history which left much of it demolished by 1800. Thomas Wedgewood lived there for a short while but in 1806 it was acquired by the famous sporting huntsman James Farquharson. The estate remains in private ownership and is not open to the public.

Thatched cottages at Tarrant Monkton.

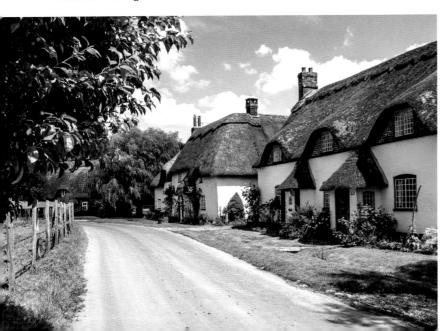

The ford at Tarrant Monkton.

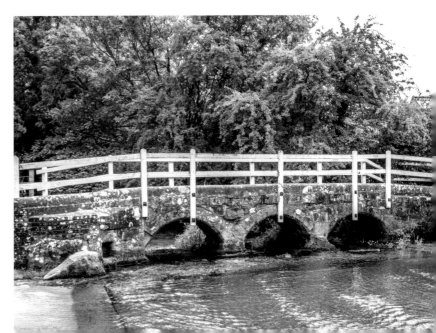

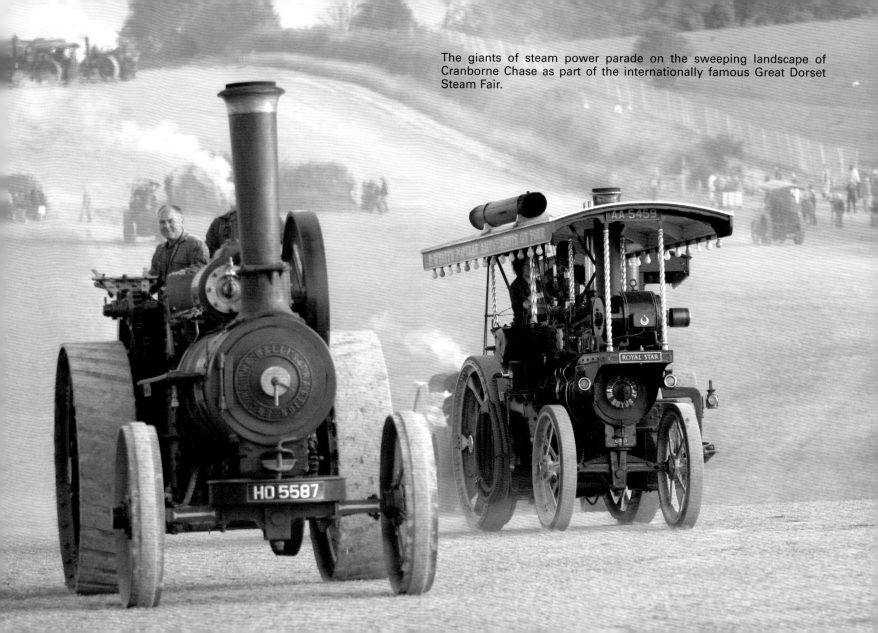

The giants of steam power parade on the sweeping landscape of Cranborne Chase as part of the internationally famous Great Dorset Steam Fair.

Tarrant Hinton

As the River Tarrant edges the Chase it runs under the road at Tarrant Hinton. This is a charming village with largely flint, brick and thatch cottages set around a fourteenth-century church. The valley setting here is green and wooded, surrounded by the rising hills towards Cranborne Chase.

Today Tarrant Hinton is famous worldwide as the site for the Great Dorset Steam Fair. Covering 600 acres, this spectacle is visited by 200,000 visitors each year and contains magnificent steam exhibits and fairgrounds from a bygone era.

Tarrant Launceston and Tarrant Monkton

Tarrant Launceston is little more than a hamlet just north of Tarrant Monkton. Tarrant Monkton however is larger with many thatched cottages, a ford and a bridge over the Tarrant.

The village features in the writings of renowned historian Sir Frederick Treves, who described the village as being 'half asleep in the sun and away from the world, a shy hamlet of thatched cottages whose walls are heavy with creepers and are hedged around by flower gardens and many orchards'. There is seemingly little I can add to that description; it is almost as though Treves has visited the village today.

Tarrant Rawston and Tarrant Rushton

The valley road through the hamlet of Tarrant Rawston follows the stream, which contains a small brick building

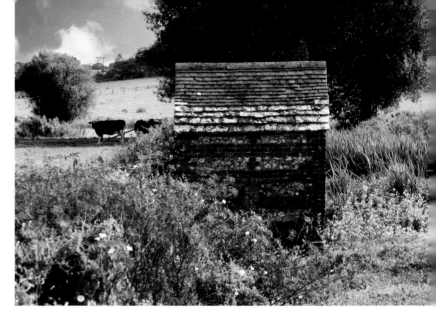

Above: The small brick building housing an undershoot water wheel which pumps water up to the adjacent farm in Tarrant Rawston.

Below: The black hangar at Tarrant Rushton, flanked by a seemingly appropriate field of 'memorial' poppies.

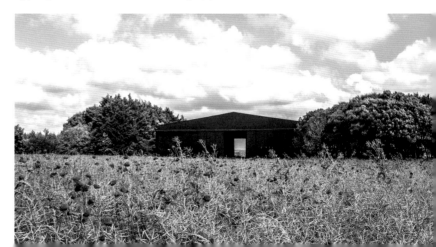

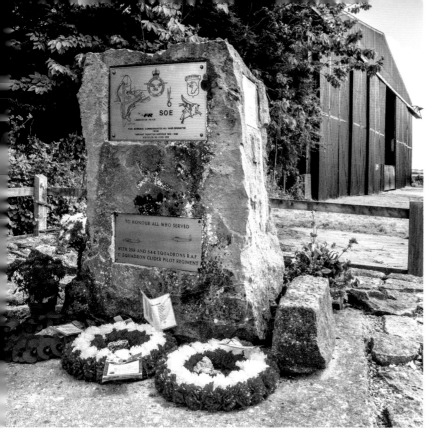

Right: The peaceful St Mary's church at Tarrant Rushton.

Left: The war memorial at Tarrant Rushton Airfield with the remaining hangar in the background.

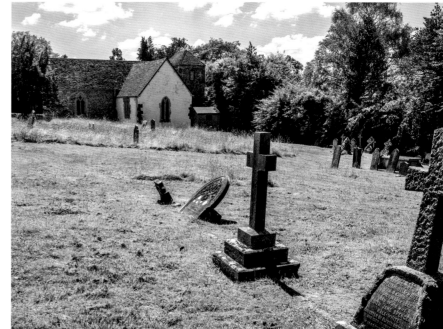

housing an undershoot waterwheel that pumps water up to the adjacent farm. The road continues over the Tarrant via a narrow bridge where the houses of Tarrant Rushton village follow the line of the river. A water-driven corn mill dating from the 1800s once worked here, but Rushton Mill ceased operation in the 1920s.

The parish church of St Mary is located in a peaceful setting to the north of the village. It is quite remarkable in that it is cruciform in shape with all arms roughly equal in length and with a small tower. It is thought the church had a leper hospital in the chancery during medieval times and a leper window is still retained in the wall.

The road rises here and passes 'The Cliff', a steep chalk escarpment, before rising to the heights where we find what remains of an important Second World War airfield. Tarrant Rushton airfield was constructed in 1942 on the site of eighteenth-century Crook Farm; the windswept agricultural land was 300 feet high above the Tarrant Valley and provided an ideal site for an airfield which suddenly became home to hundreds of airmen and their support staff arriving from all over Britain and the Commonwealth countries.

From this lonely airfield, with its 1-mile-long main runway, left Halifax and Sterling bombers on sorties far into occupied Europe. It was also a main base for Glider pilots whose enormous Hamilcar and Horsa gliders, towed by Halifax bombers, carried tanks and arms into Europe for land-based troops and members of the French Resistance. Secret agents from the Special Operations Executive were also flown out of Tarrant Rushton and dropped into enemy territory causing the airfield to be known as the 'secret airfield'.

It played an important role in the Normandy landings in 1944, with the first troops to land having been flown out from Tarrant Rushton. The airfield also played a major part in the Arnhem and Rhine Crossing operations

After the war the airfield became the home of aviation pioneer Sir Alan Cobham's Flight Refuelling Ltd, where it became involved in the Berlin Airlift with Lancastrians and Lancasters flying over 4,000 sorties out of Tarrant Rushton.

As the home of Flight Refuelling Ltd, the airfield saw the perfection of the in-flight refuelling system, refurbishment of F84 and T33 aircraft for the Belgian Airforce, conversion of Meteor jets to pilotless drone aircraft and many international aviation-based research projects before its eventual closure on 30 September 1980. Sir Alan Cobham died in 1973 and rests with his wife, Gladys, in the churchyard of St Mary's, close to the airfield which played such a great part in his exceptional life.

A memorial to all those who served at the airfield is located by the roadside next to one of the surviving hangars.

On a more personal note, Tarrant Rushton airfield was always known to me as a boy when I cycled from my Wimborne home to see what was going on there in the 1950s. From the top of the hill I would gaze in awe at the dark shapes of the famous wartime bombers lined up in the distance and visualise all the clandestine wartime operations which went on there. Little did I know that in the autumn of 1960 I would walk through the entrance to the airfield to receive my first interview, which launched a forty-four-year career in Sir Alan Cobham's company. I even had the experience of flying from Tarrant Rushton in the company's twin engine Piper Aztec before the flying operations were transferred to Hurn, now Bournemouth International Airport. Strangely, my career ended on 30 September 2004, twenty-four years to the day that Tarrant Rushton airfield also retired.

Tarrant Keyneston

The River Tarrant flows under the main Wimborne to Blandford road at Tarrant Keyneston, which takes its name from the lords of the manor in the twelfth century. Here the valley road also crosses the main road beside the inn with the fascinating name of The True Lovers Knot.

It is not known precisely how this intriguing pub name came about, but locals have for years told a consistent tale of a tragic love affair. The inn originally served travellers who stopped at the nearby toll gate, managed by the lord of the manor. It was at the toll gate that the landlord's son met the lord's daughter. They fell instantly in love but continued their relationship in secret in fear of the lord not approving of his daughter's relationship with a commoner. When he eventually found out about his daughter's relationship, she was forbidden to see the boy ever again and plans were made for her to be sent away. Overcome with grief, the girl hanged herself on a tree in the estate and soon afterwards the young man also hanged himself from the same tree. The landlord of the inn was a widower and found it impossible to carry on without his son; he also hanged himself from the same tree. From that time the inn was referred to as The True Lovers Knot. As depicted in the pub sign, the knot has three loops, one for each person who died and when correctly tied has a

Right: The True Lovers Knot at Tarrant Keyneston.

Left: Cottages at Tarrant Keyneston.

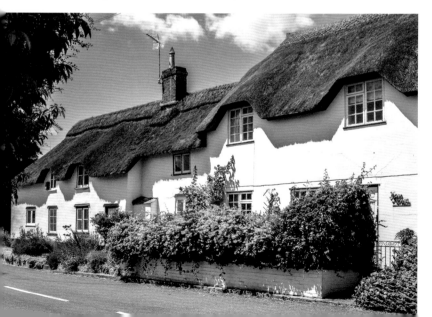

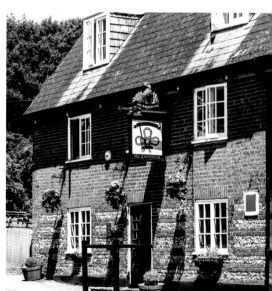

heart in the centre. As a spooky ending to the tale, it is said the inn remains haunted by the landlord from this tragic tale to this day.

Tarrant Crawford

Tarrant Crawford is the most southerly of the Tarrant villages and is near the River Tarrant's confluence with the Dorset Stour near Spetisbury. Tarrant Crawford Bridge crosses the Stour, replacing what was once a ford.

There is little trace of it today, but near the small parish church of St Mary was once the site of one of the richest nunneries in England, established around 1100 by the Lord of the Manor but later re-founded by Bishop Richard Poore. Bishop Poore was

Tarrant Crawford village.

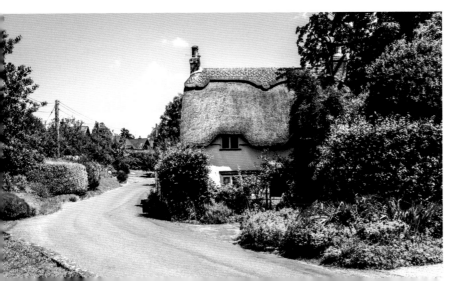

born in the village and went on to become builder of Salisbury Cathedral in addition to the bishop of Chichester and Durham. He later returned to Tarrant Crawford and was buried in the abbey in 1237.

The village is also famous for its contribution to having had one of the first books written in the English language, written in Tarrant abbey. It is known as the *Ancrene Riwle* and details a set of rules for women who wished to become nuns. It has been described as an example of the very best of eloquent English prose and is thought to have been written by Tarrant Crawford's own Richard Poore.

All that remains of the ancient abbey today.

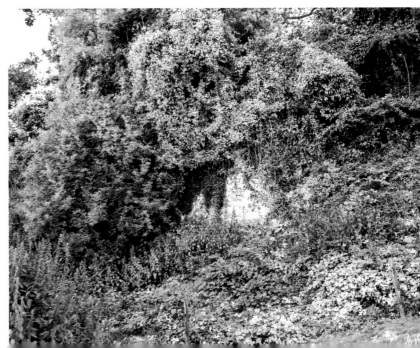

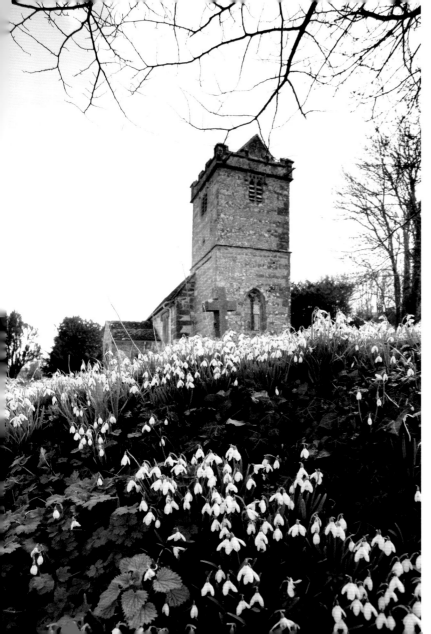

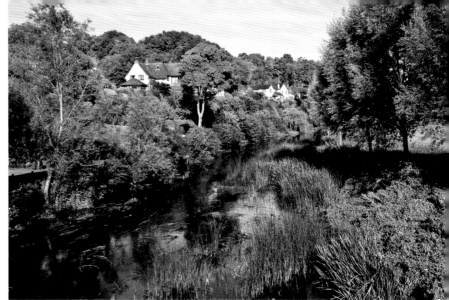

Above: The River Stour at Spetisbury viewed from Tarrant Crawford Bridge.

Left: Tarrant Crawford's church of St Mary is famous for its seasonal display of snowdrops.

TOLLARD ROYAL

Tollard Royal is sometimes called the capital of the Chase, set in a beautiful wooded landscape. It is here the valley road separates Dorset from Wiltshire.

The word 'Tollard' in Celtic terms suggests a 'valley location' and the word 'Royal' links to King John, who acquired the tenure to the area and the hunting rights of Cranborne Chase.

It is said that King John slept at Tollard Royal during his hunting excursions on the Chase. In fact, near the church is the site of a royal hunting lodge with parts dating from the thirteenth century. It is named King John's House, was restored by Gen. Augustus Pitt Rivers and is now in private ownership.

The village inn, The King John Inn, is also named after the hunting King, and was first opened in 1859.

Nearby is the private Ashcombe Estate and the magnificent Ashcombe House; the home from 1930 to 1945 of photographer and designer Cecil Beaton, who leased the house from its then owner for a nominal rent in return for carrying out renovations. During his time there, Cecil Beaton entertained lavishly and his many visitors included prominent artists and actors. When his lease expired in 1945 it is said Beaton was heartbroken to leave the house but found a new home at Broadchalke on the other side of the Chase.

Ashcombe house later became the home of film director Guy Ritchie and his, now estranged wife, Madonna.

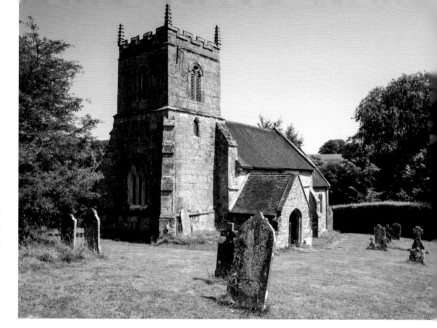

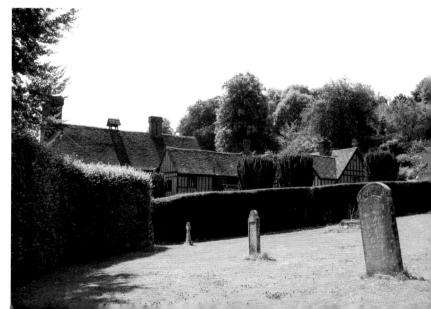

Above: Tollard Royal's church of St Peter ad Vincula.

Below: King John's House as seen from the churchyard.

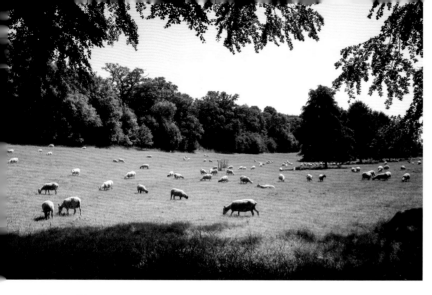

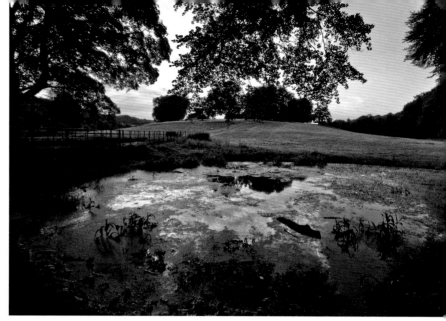

Above: Sheep grazing in the lush valley setting at Tollard Royal.

Above right: Evening landscape near Tollard Royal.

Below right: Winter scene at Tollard Royal's pond.

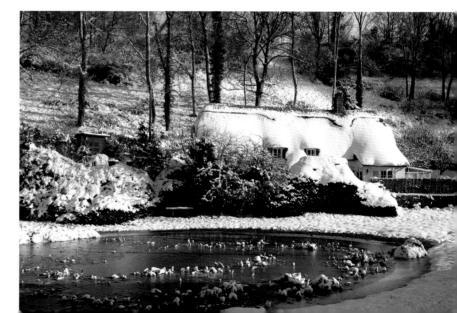

WIMBORNE MINSTER

Roger Holman and I are both Wimborne people, so this has to be the most difficult section we have to cover. Having natural attachments to the area, our photography here has been somewhat extensive over the years. Many residents will no doubt remember our audio-visual show *The Changing Face of Wimborne* and our photographic support of the model town and the Tivoli cinema during their days of demise and subsequent resurrection. It therefore becomes too easy for us to maintain our enthusiasm for Wimborne and all that it provides. Therefore, we hope to provide a balance with elsewhere in the landscapes of Cranborne Chase. Should we fail to achieve this I trust we can both be pardoned and not suddenly find ourselves in the stocks at Wimborne St Giles or indeed as prisoners in Cranborne Manor.

This historical market town finds itself on the northern shores of the River Stour, which has journeyed here from its source in Wiltshire, whereas the River Allen, which owes its source to the chalk downland of Cranborne Chase, flows directly through the very centre of the town, passing both its historic and modern-day styles.

Who can say which is Wimborne's river? Certainly the Stour has caused much flooding for Wimborne, but equally it is the larger river of the two and must provide long-term residents of Wimborne with rich memories. For me as a child at Little Canford it was an adventurous place to be, providing my first experiences of fishing and many attempts at crossings by reed raft. Later in life, my office window overlooked the river for almost forty years. Although, I can honestly say while I have experienced the Stour in all its glory over many years and seasons we must not forget the Allen. This charming river has provided three working mills for the town. From its origins as a clear chalk stream, it is still home to rare species of crayfish, wild trout and water vole, not to mention the wild flower habitats along its banks and the springtime abundance of craysfoot.

Without doubt the centrepiece of Wimborne is the minster from which it takes its name. From whichever direction you enter the town the twin towers are instantly recognisable.

The minster is dedicated to St Cuthburga, sister to the King of the West Saxons. It was St Cuthburga who founded a Benedictine nunnery here in AD 705, housing more than 500 women. The nunnery was destroyed by the Danes during one of their expeditions to Wessex in 1013. The present minster stands on the same site.

In 871, Alfred the Great buried his brother, Ethelred (not to be confused with Ethelred the Unready), in the minster. Ethelred was mortally wounded during a battle at Martin on the edge of Cranborne Chase.

In 1043, Edward the Confessor founded a college of secular or non-monastic canons here and in support of this college the Normans built much of the minster as we see it today; it even escaped severe damage during the Civil War. One of the minster's most significant features is the Chained Library, one of only four surviving in the world. Raleigh's *History of the World* is here, written in 1638 and with around 100 pages burned through and carefully repaired by one Matthew Prior, who, it is said, fell asleep while reading it by the aid of a lighted candle which toppled with disastrous effect.

Wimborne is an enchanting little town with its ancient and more recent history revealed in the Priest's House Museum. Over the years it has received its changes with dignity, if occasionally somewhat controversially. However, the town we see today has emerged with the characterful streets harmonising gently with the new, providing open space for its famous folk festival and a colourful environment enriched by its ever-present award-winning 'Wimborne in Bloom' flower displays.

It is quite surprising to learn that over the years the town has provided a home and education for many notable residents, from the infamous smuggler and entrepreneur Isaac Gulliver, Montague John Druitt, a major suspect in the 'Jack the Ripper' case, and Dorset's most famous writer, Thomas Hardy, to the inventor of the World Wide Web, Sir Tim Berners-Lee and Professor George Gray, a resident of Wimborne for twenty-five years, whose pioneering research into liquid crystal technology has transformed the world of communication including telephones, computers and televisions.

Charles Castleman was also an important figurehead for the town; he built the railway which connected Wimborne and Dorset to the wider national rail network (now of course long gone following the fall of the 'Beeching Axe' in the 1960s).

Musician and guitarist Robert Fripp of King Crimson fame resided for many years in Wimborne, calling it 'the centre of the universe'. Al Stewart, singer-songwriter famed for his 1976 hit *Year of the Cat* was also brought up in the town and *Dambusters* actor Richard Todd was educated at the Grammar School, as was screenwriter, actor and director Lionel Jeffries. Additionally, star of many films and TV series, Michael Medwin OBE still lives in Wimborne. Another renowned Wimborne name from the silver screen is Margaret James, who remains the only surviving member of the cast of the classic movie *Brief Encounter*. The famous wartime voice of BBC announcer Stuart Hibberd MBE will long be remembered for his most eloquent news broadcasts, and although born in nearby Broadstone he was also educated at Wimborne Grammar School.

Perhaps not always so much appreciated is Wimborne's connection with Australia. Lt William Cox was born in the town in 1764 and became responsible for building the first road across the Blue Mountains of Australia, contributing much to the development of the new colony.

Today the town emerges from its cultural past with its history well documented and displayed in the Priest's House Museum, a fine restored Art Deco Tivoli theatre and cinema together with Walford Mill on the River Allen, now a prominent art and craft centre.

We cannot leave Wimborne without mentioning the famous model town which opened on a site just off the Cornmarket in 1951 and became an instant tourist attraction. It is a 1:10 scale model town of Wimborne as it was in the 1950s, complete with shops displaying their wares in the miniature windows. Despite its popularity, the model town changed ownership over the years until falling into the hands of a property developer. The models soon declined but were saved from the bulldozer in the 1980s by a group of townsfolk determined to see it restored and relocated. The developer agreed to give the models to the town and Sir Michael Hanham provided space on his estate land where the model town now lives again thanks to the efforts of many volunteers who moved and rebuilt the successful tourist attraction visitors and residents can now enjoy.

Wimborne's history is not complete without reference to Deans Court, home to the Hanham family since 1548. The house was originally thought to be the eleventh-century deanery to the minster at the time of Edward the Confessor. However, following recent investigations it is now considered to be much older, with the Hall House being the house of the Abbess who was installed to run the nunnery. During recent dredging of the monastic fishpond Saxon artefacts were found, confirming that the Hall House and monastic pond may well be Saxon and date from the eighth century. Following the 1547 Dissolution of the Chantries Act the house and manor of Wimborne were granted to Sir John Hanham, then MP for Poole. The Hanham family have lived there ever since. The interesting gardens with their wide selection of specimen trees and attractive walled garden are open as part of the National Gardens Scheme several times each year and it was my privilege to be asked by Lady Hanham to photograph the grounds shortly before her death in 2007. At that time I remember a very interesting afternoon with her husband, Sir Michael, sharing his aviation reminiscences of being a flight engineer on Halifax and Lancasters and later as a flight planner based at Heathrow. Sadly, Sir Michael died in 2009.

The Cutherberga window in Wimborne minster showing Cutherberga holding a model of the minster as she stands alongside St Luke.

The twin towers of Wimborne minster across the Stour water meadows in winter.

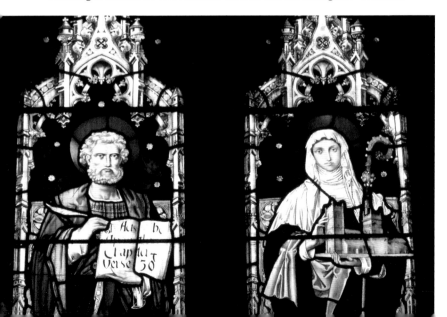

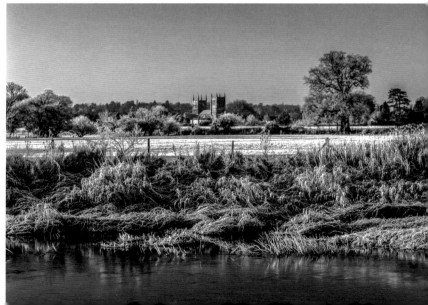

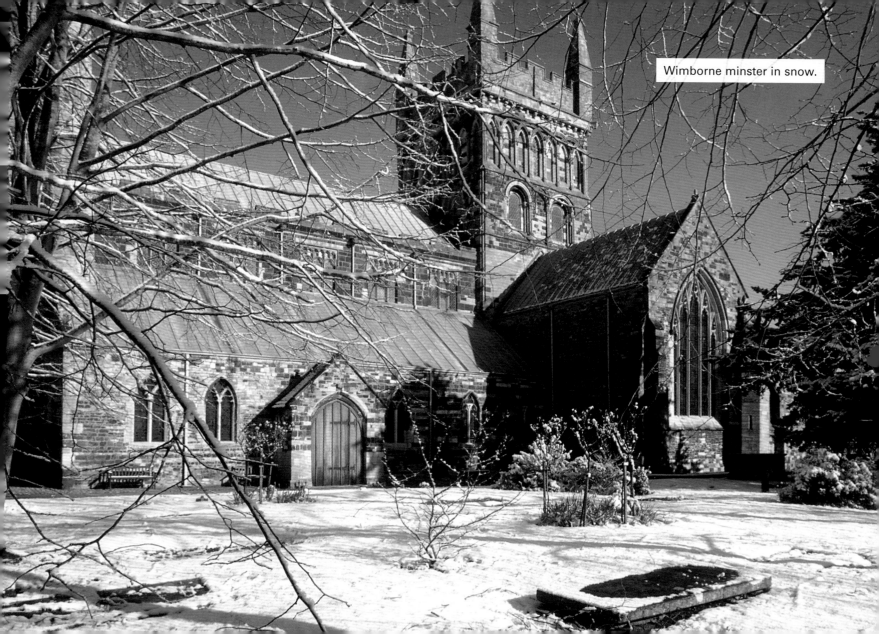

Wimborne minster in snow.

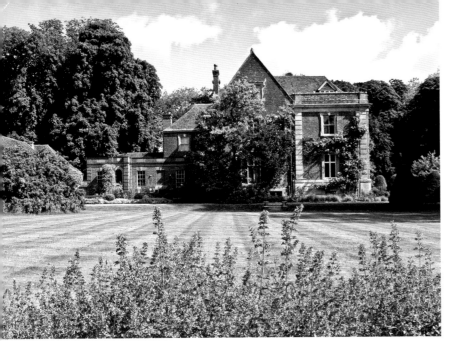

Right: The Herb Garden at Deans Court.

Left: Deans Court House.

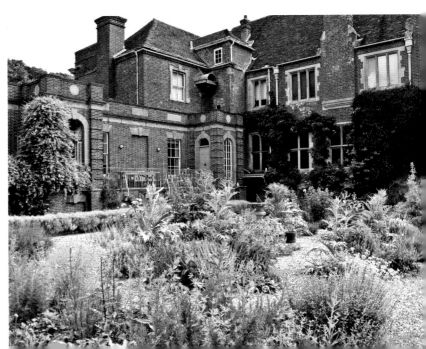

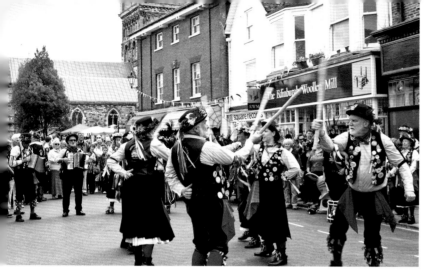

Above: The colourful Wimborne Folk Festival.

Below: The model town today showing the high street as it was in the 1950s.

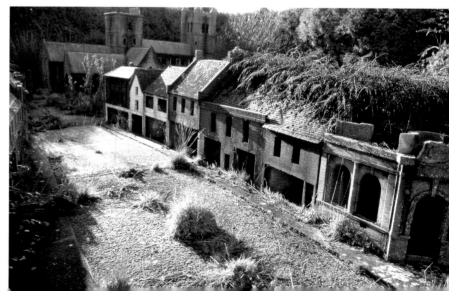

Above: Wimborne's model town on the new site in a garden setting.

Below: The model town before relocation and restoration.

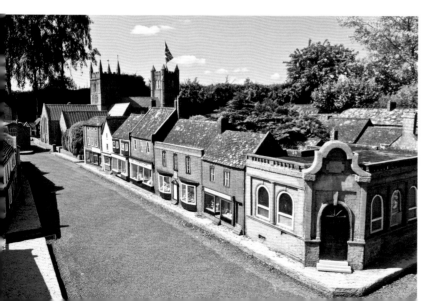

WIMBORNE ST GILES

Wimborne St Giles is in my opinion one of Dorset's most quintessential villages and takes its name from the meadow stream or the River Allen from Old English *winn* and *burna*. St Giles refers to the dedication of the church, St Giles being an eighth-century hermit of French origin.

Secluded and surrounded by Chase woodland, it has undoubtedly benefited from being an estate village with a planned and maintained character. Located just a few miles north of Wimborne Minster, the church, alms houses and village school all look out across a village green with the ever-present village stocks very much in evidence. With the River Allen running close by, a perfect rural atmosphere can be found here and the village hall has an enviable reputation for cream teas on Sunday afternoons.

The River Allen rises nearby and flows through the estate at Wimborne St Giles.

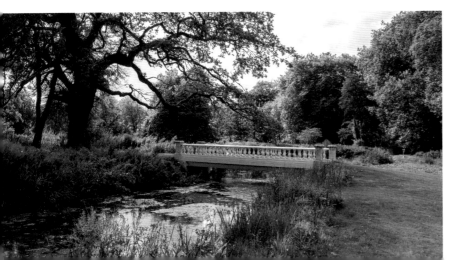

The village remains the seat of the earls of Shaftesbury and their St Giles House is nearby. Their manorial estate has been in the same family ownership by marriage and inheritance since the Norman Conquest. The current title holders, the Ashley-Coopers, have in fact been in residence on the estate since the fifteenth century.

There is so much that can be written in history about this family and the estate it would require a full chapter on its own, but we cannot pass through the history of Wimborne St Giles without mention of two earls of Shaftesbury who have in some way significantly contributed to our lifestyles today. The first being Anthony Ashley (1551–1628), who it is said was something of a character and is thought to have introduced cabbages to England from Holland. This explains why carvings of cabbages appear on monuments at Wimborne St Giles. In 1624 he had built the row of red-brick almshouses to accommodate eleven poor widows of the parish, which can still be seen today and remain a significant feature of the village. Two generations later, his grandson, Anthony Ashley-Cooper, was made the 1st Earl of Shaftesbury at the time of the coronation of Charles II.

However, it is perhaps the 7th Earl of Shaftesbury (1801–55) that we are possibly more familiar with. He was a prominent politician of the Victorian era and a significant leader in social reform.

It was this Anthony Ashley-Cooper who fought for the abolition of child labour and a universal education for children. As one of the founders of Great Ormond Street Children's Hospital, he was also a great philanthropist and his many legacies are still of benefit to us all today. We are reminded of his generosity and charitable works by Alfred Gilbert's life-size statue of *Christian*

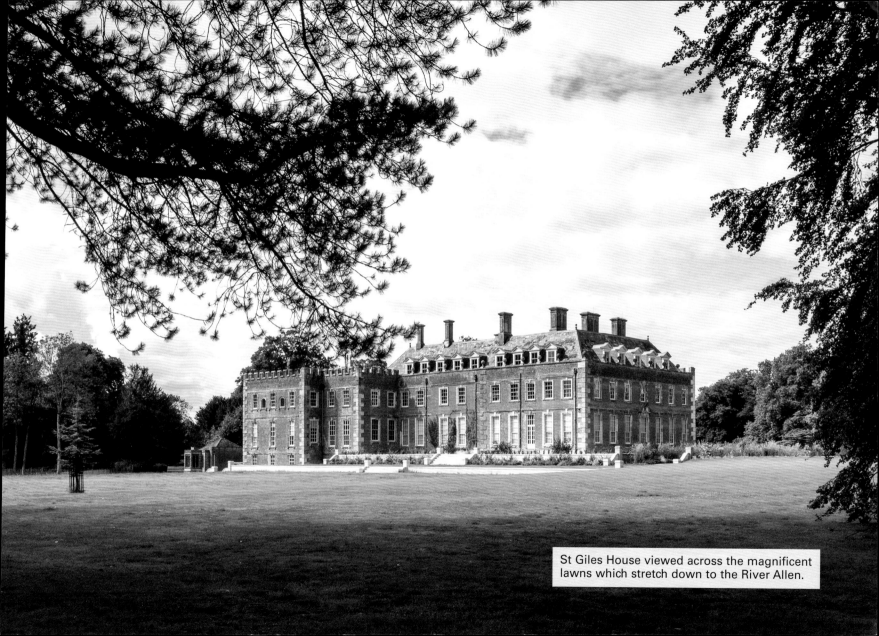
St Giles House viewed across the magnificent lawns which stretch down to the River Allen.

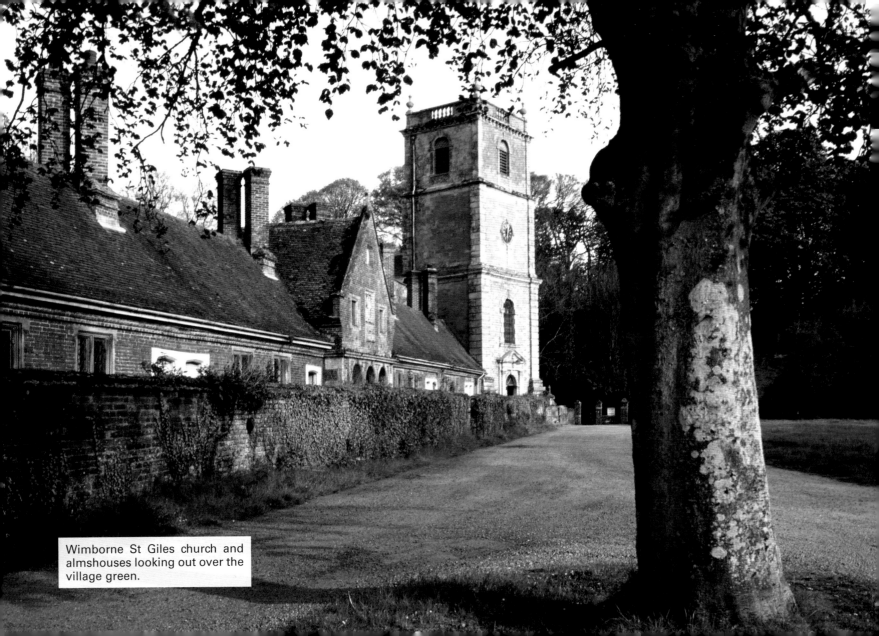

Wimborne St Giles church and almshouses looking out over the village green.

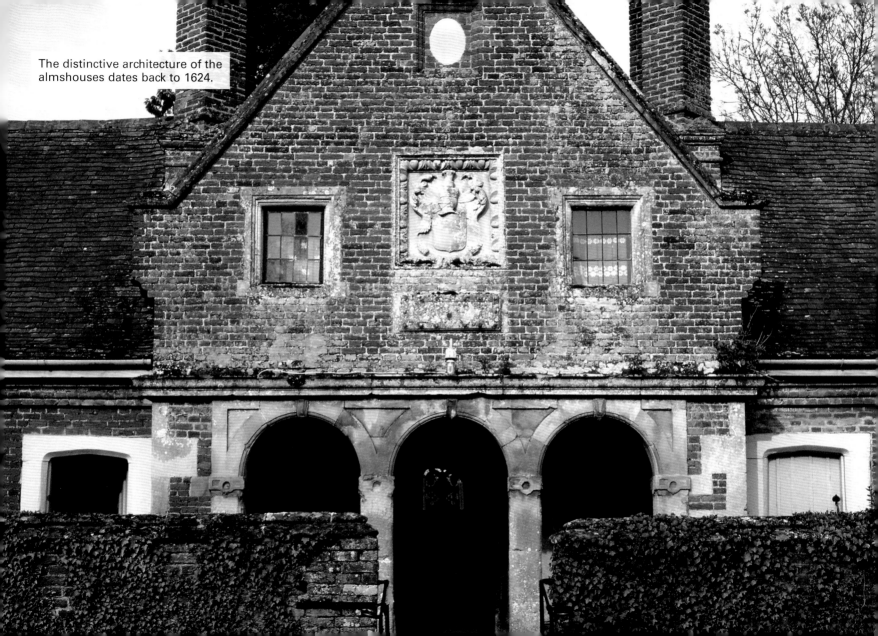

The distinctive architecture of the almshouses dates back to 1624.

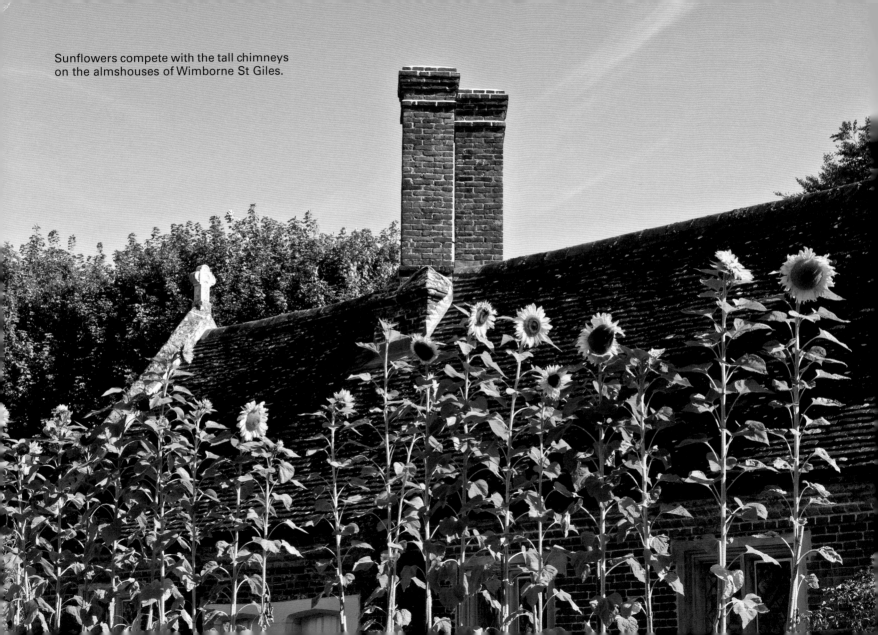

Sunflowers compete with the tall chimneys on the almshouses of Wimborne St Giles.

Love in London's Piccadilly Circus. Mistakenly known as *Eros*, it was unveiled in 1893 in tribute to the 7th Earl of Shaftesbury's philanthropic work with the arrow pointing towards Wimborne St Giles in his honour.

The handsome church overlooking the village green was originally built in 1732 by the Bastard brothers on the site of a Tudor church but was largely destroyed by fire in 1908. The current church was redesigned by Ninian Comper in a style complimentary to the surviving eighteenth-century work.

The village stocks.

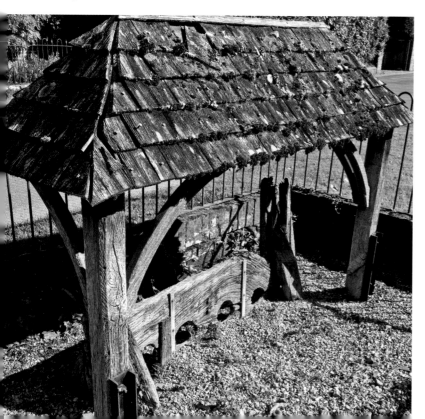

WIN GREEN

This famous hill, with its familiar landmark clump of trees, is the highest point in Cranborne Chase but lies on the Wiltshire side of the boundary. At 910 feet there are panoramic views from its summit, where the entire Chase can be seen with distant landscapes stretching as far as the New Forest and the Hampshire Solent in one direction and to Dorset's Purbeck Hills in the other, with Wiltshire and Somerset to the west beyond the ancient town of Shaftesbury.

When the traveller from Shaftesbury rises to the heights above the infamous Zig Zag Hill reaching the expansive wide open landscape of Charlton Down, Win Green immediately comes into view, riding on the curves of the downland, perhaps one of the most significant symbols of Cranborne Chase.

From Win Green, the Ox Drove can be accessed for more than 10 miles. This is one of the great cross-country ridgeways which have been used by man for centuries. In fact it is not difficult to visualise a rural character from one of Hardy's novels surrounded by a herd of sheep traversing the spectacle of Win Green en route to Salisbury or another field along the Chalke valley.

Among the trees of Win Green, where the wind whistles through the canopy of branches reaching towards the sky, where buzzards and falcons ride on the thermals in search of prey, it can seem a magical place, if somewhat eerie. Here, thoughts of ancient rituals and culture spring to mind as the landscape offers its secrets so steeped in legend.

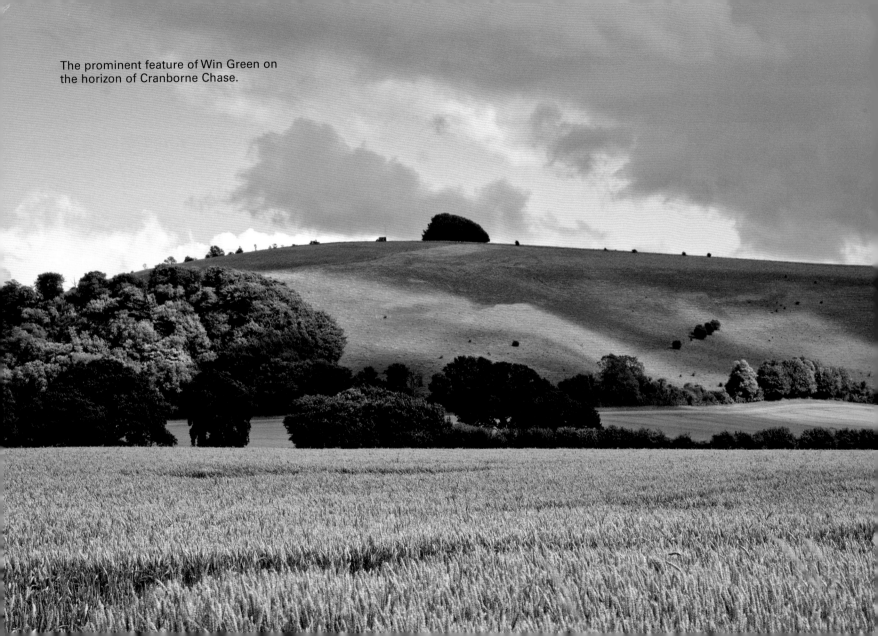

The prominent feature of Win Green on
the horizon of Cranborne Chase.

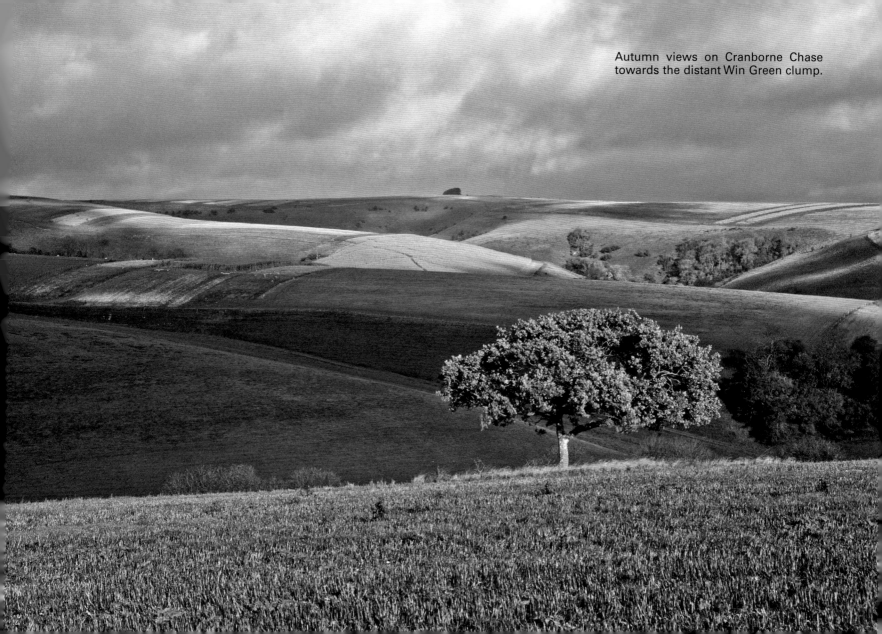

Autumn views on Cranborne Chase towards the distant Win Green clump.

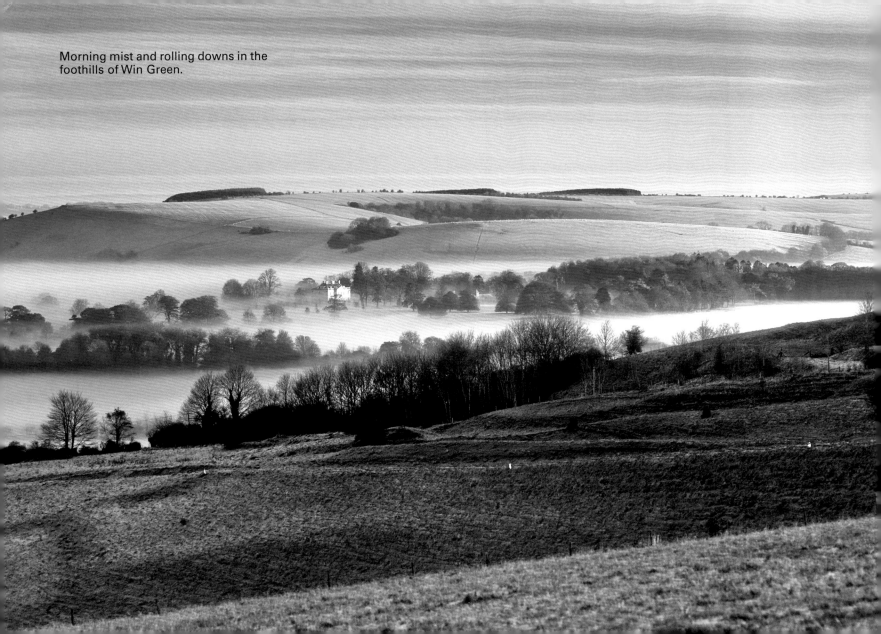

Morning mist and rolling downs in the foothills of Win Green.

WITCHAMPTON AND THE RIVER ALLEN

Witchampton has been described as one of the most beautiful villages in the county and winds its way above the east-facing banks of the River Allen just 5 miles north of Wimborne Minster. The timber-framed thatched cottages make this an idyllic and traditional village scene. Much of this preserved location is due to the control of the Crichel Estate, which owned almost every property in the village until the mid-twentieth century.

There are said to be signs of a Roman vineyard in the neighbouring grounds of the church, thus providing a link to the village's ancient history. Domesday records reveal two flour mills along Witchampton's stretch of the Allen, one of which, to the northeast of the village, became a paper mill in the early eighteenth century and remained in operation until the twentieth century.

The parish church is dedicated to St Mary, St Cuthberga and All Saints. St Cuthberga was the founder of Wimborne minster and she can be seen dressed as an abbess holding a crosier in one hand and a miniature Wimborne minster in the other; her statue stands over the Arts & Crafts style lych-gate. The church underwent major changes between 1832 and 1840 and little of the original church remains, other than the bowl of the thirteenth-century font and the fifteenth-century tower.

The River Allen is a pure chalk stream which rises near Monkton up Wimborne and flows for around 13 miles through rich water meadows, arable fields, occasional copse and riverside trees on its way to meet the Dorset Stour just outside Wimborne. Here the two rivers combine until the Stour joins the Avon from Wiltshire to meet the sea at Christchurch.

Chalk streams are some of the richest river habitats for wildlife and the River Allen is noted for holding the highest population of the native white-clawed crayfish. It is also renowned for wild brown trout and water vole.

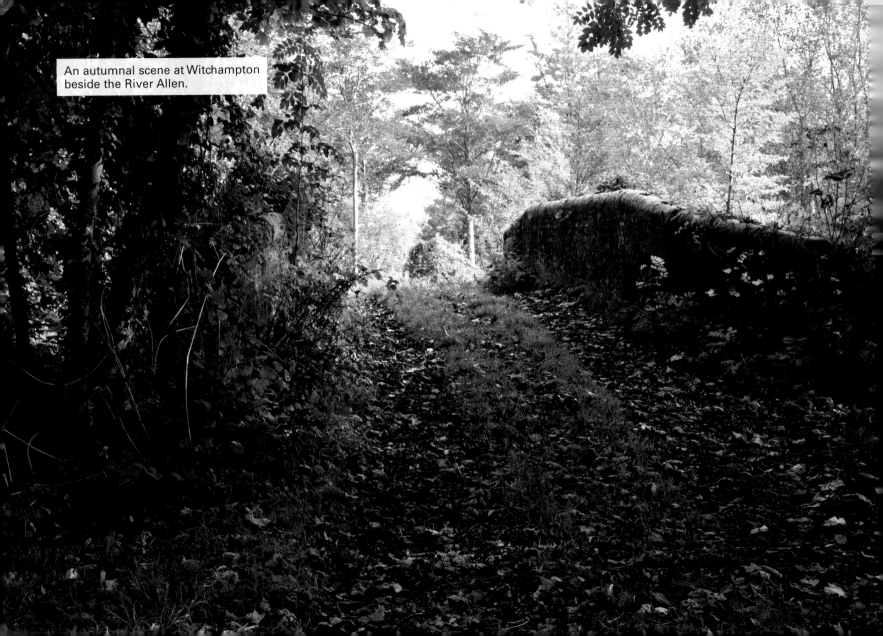

An autumnal scene at Witchampton beside the River Allen.

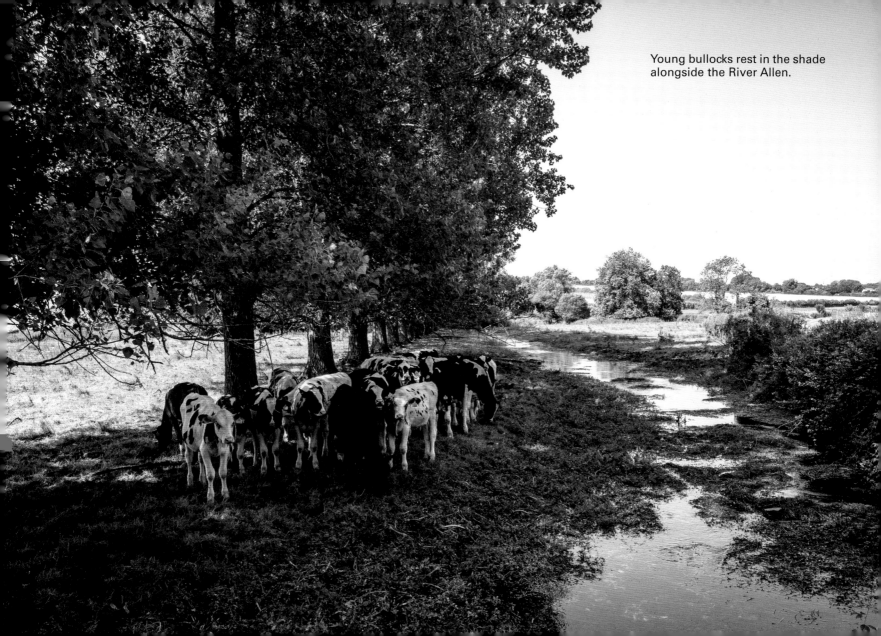

Young bullocks rest in the shade alongside the River Allen.

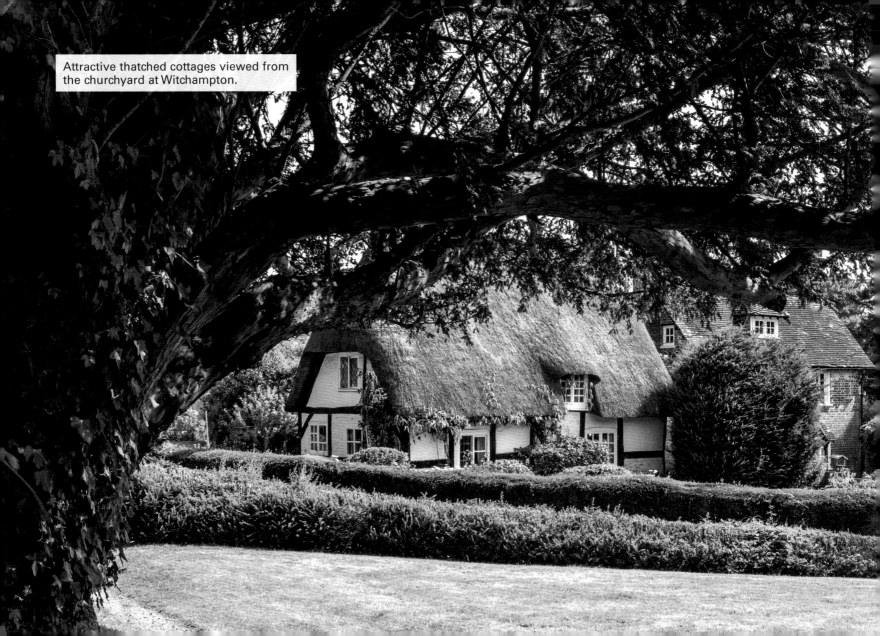

Attractive thatched cottages viewed from the churchyard at Witchampton.

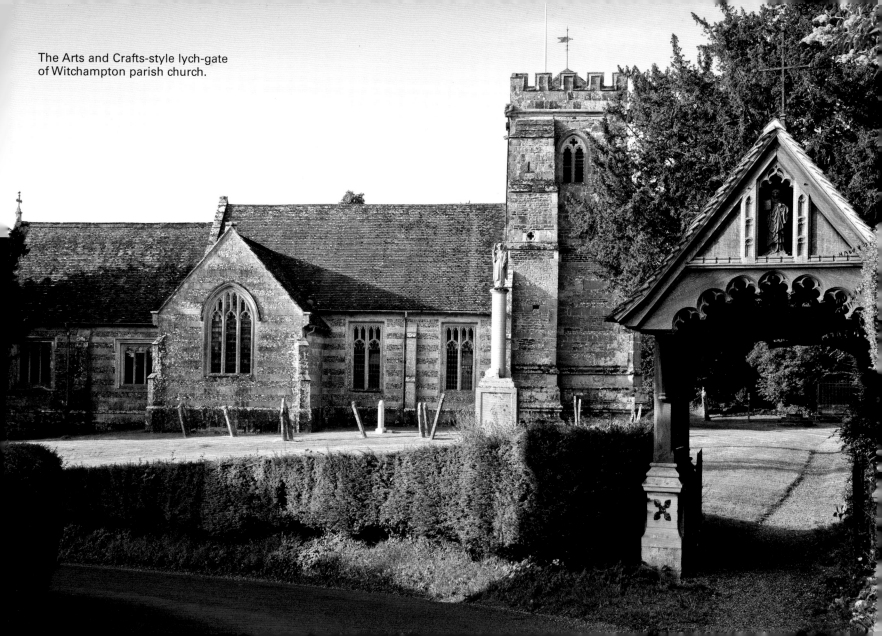

The Arts and Crafts-style lych-gate of Witchampton parish church.

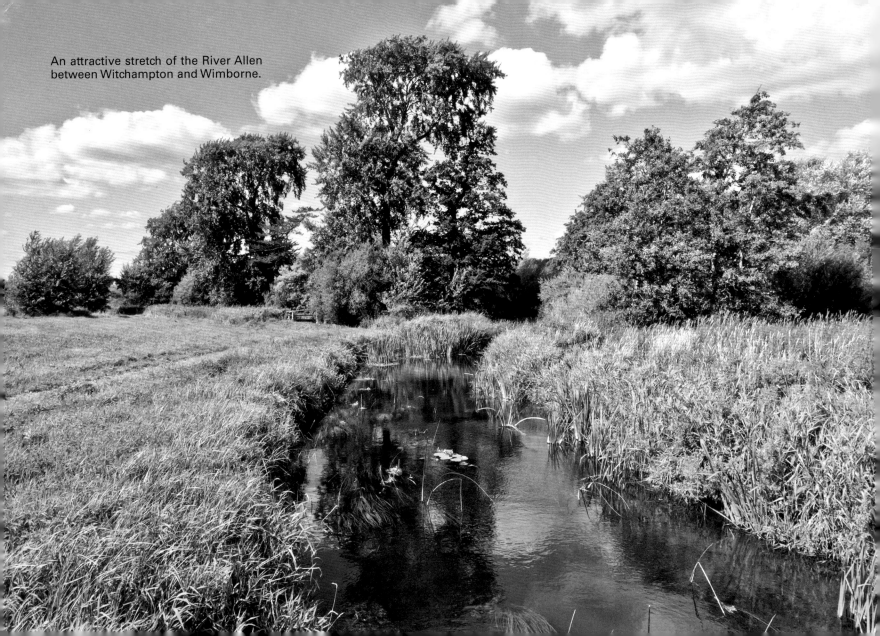

An attractive stretch of the River Allen
between Witchampton and Wimborne.

ACKNOWLEDGEMENTS

Indulging in landscape photography is normally quite a solitary experience, but I am most grateful when photographing this book to have again been accompanied by my good friend Roger Holman. We have worked together on previous books and audio-visual projects since the late 1960s, and I am always grateful for Roger's intimate knowledge of Dorset, continued enthusiasm and persistent searching for the best light and composition. One day I hope to match his ability for early morning expeditions into a pre-sunrise landscape.

I must also thank my wife for her tolerance and understanding of just why it is so necessary to spend many hours working on a computer or traversing the countryside with a camera.

Finally and by no means least, this book would not have been possible without certain permissions to photograph and I am most grateful to all those who have been so generous and supportive of the book to make such arrangements possible.

David Blake and Harry Bell – Cranborne Chase Area of Outstanding Natural Beauty (AONB)

Robert Gray – National Trust, Kingston Lacy

Carol Cross – Larmer Tree Gardens

Charlotte Spender – Estate Secretary, Wilton House

Madeline Andrews – Rockbourne Roman villa

Sir Michael Hanham and Jonathan Cornish – Deans Court Estate, Wimborne

Lord Shaftesbury and Catharine Burchell – St Giles House, Wimborne St Giles

Luke Winter and Pascale Barnes – Cranborne Ancient Technology Centre

English Heritage Staff at South West Office (Old Wardour Castle)

Museum Staff of Shaftesbury Abbey Museum & Gardens

Tony Bates for his natural history expertise and photography

Kay Browning for her image of the Fovant Badges (an image which eluded us during our many photography trips)

Lucy Nankivell for proofreading and correcting my original text

FURTHER INFORMATION

For further information about Cranborne Chase and some of the locations featured in the book, the following websites will provide all you need to know:

Cranborne Chase
www.ccwwdaonb.org.uk

Kingston Lacy and Badbury Rings
www.nationaltrust.org.uk/kingstonlacy

The Royal Signals Museum, Blandford Forum
royalsignalsmuseum.co.uk/WebSite

Compton Abbas Airfield
www.comptonabbasairfield.co.uk

Cranborne Manor and Gardens
www.cranborne.co.uk

Cranborne Ancient Technology Centre
www.ancienttechnologycentre.co.uk

Nature Reserves on Cranborne Chase
www.dorsetwildlifetrust.org.uk
www.wiltshirewildlife.org

Larmer Tree Gardens
www.larmertree.co.uk

Salisbury Cathedral
www.salisburycathedral.org.uk/visit

The Nadder Valley
www.discovernadder.org.uk

Old Wardour Castle
www.english-heritage.org.uk/daysout/properties/old-wardour-castle

Fovant Badges
www.fovantbadges.com

Wilton House
www.wiltonhouse.co.uk

Rockbourne Roman villa
www.hants.gov.uk/rockbourne-roman-villa

Shaftesbury Abbey Gardens
shaftesburyabbey.org.uk

Shaftesbury Gold Hill
www.goldhillmuseum.org.uk

Garston Wood
www.rspb.org.uk

Great Dorset Steam Fair
www.gdsf.co.uk

Wimborne Minster
www.wimborneminster.org.uk

Wimborne's Priest House Museum
www.priest-house.co.uk

Wimborne's Model Town
www.wimborne-modeltown.com

Wimborne Folk Festival
www.wimbornefolk.co.uk

Deans Court, Wimborne
www.deanscourt.org/Deans_Court/Deans_Court.html

St Giles House, Wimborne St Giles
www.shaftesburyestates.com

BIBLIOGRAPHY

Barrett, Professor John (ed.), Richard Bradley (ed.), Martin Green (ed.)

Landscape, Monuments and Society: The Prehistory of Cranborne Chase (Cambridge University Press, First edition 18 Jun 2009).

Hawkins, Desmond, *Cranborne Chase* (Victor Gollancz Ltd, First edition 13 Mar 1980).

Sumner, Heywood, *The Ancient Earthworks of Cranborne Chase* (Sutton Publishing Ltd, New edition 30 Jun 1988).